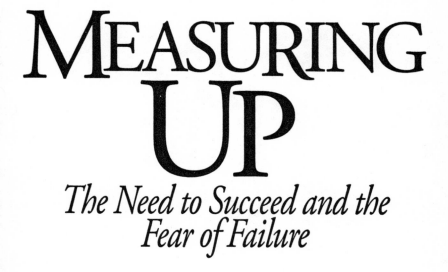

MEASURING UP

The Need to Succeed and the Fear of Failure

STUART BRISCOE
KNUTE LARSON
LARRY OSBORNE

MULTNOMAH BOOKS

MEASURING UP
© 1993 by Christianity Today, Inc.

Published by Multnomah Press Books
Questar Publishers, Inc.
Sisters, Oregon

Printed in the United States of America

International Standard Book Number: 0-88070-597-3

Most Scripture quotations are from the *New International Version* (©1973, 1978, 1984
by the International Bible Society; used by permission of Zondervan Publishing House).

93 94 95 96 97 98 99 00 01 — 10 9 8 7 6 5 4 3 2 1

Contents

Introduction

Our high school basketball team won only one game, losing sixteen. I was starting guard for our runt of a team (the tallest player was only six-feet tall), which dwelled in the cellar of the smallest school division (Class B) in South Dakota. We played rural towns with Indian names like Woonsocket and Iroquois, and got ambushed by each of them, occasionally by thirty points or more.

Early in that season, losing didn't feel so bad; we knew most of the season was still before us, and winning was just a game away. But as the season wore on and victory kept eluding us, an invisible gloom settled over the team.

Before each game we'd slap each other on the back and talk

tough. The adrenalin would rise. Emotionally charged, we'd exit the locker room and head for the basketball court — only to get pummeled, often humiliated, by our opponents. During the first half of the season, we had lots of heart but no talent. The last half we possessed neither.

Our lone win came near the end of that long season but tasted bittersweet. We managed to squeak out a one-point win against a team that also hadn't won a game all season.

Sports is about winning and losing. Though serving God isn't ultimately about keeping score, sometimes it feels that way. We pastors get discouraged by setback after setback, so that even victories can feel bittersweet. We want desperately to succeed, but we live with a nagging fear of failure.

Then there come those winning seasons, when attendance and offerings assure us of our success — until we hear Jesus' words about faithfulness. Then we wonder once more what success and failure look like.

In this third book of Mastering Ministry's Pressure Points series, three pastors offer their reflections on success and failure. Their sixty collective years of local church ministry, fired by the heat of everyday pressures, have given them keen insight into how we can measure what we're accomplishing.

Stuart Briscoe

Stuart Briscoe received an early lesson about success from a legend.

"I was a small boy in England," he once said, "when Donald Grey Barnhouse spoke in a tent at a Keswick Convention. He was an imposing figure, and without preamble he suddenly shouted, 'The way to up is down!' The staid Britishers fluttered. Then with even more drama and volume he said, 'And the way to down is up!' His text was 1 Peter 5:5–6: 'All of you, clothe yourselves in humility toward one another, because "God opposes the proud but gives grace to the humble." Humble yourselves, therefore, under God's mighty hand, that he may lift you up in due time.' Even to a young, disinterested boy, his message got across. It's a lesson I still struggle to learn." Still, he's learned it well.

Stuart started out as a banking official in his native England. He went from there to full-time ministry, working with Capernwray Missionary Fellowship of Torchbearers, traveling around the world as an itinerant missionary. In 1970 he accepted the call to pastor Elmbrook Church in Waukesha, Wisconsin, a suburb of Milwaukee. After twenty-three years of his leadership, Elmbrook Church has grown to more than 6,000 in weekly worship services.

Stuart enters the pulpit each week with a simple prayer such as: "Lord, here I am. As far as I can tell, I've tried to fill my sack with good seed. I've done my homework, I think my attitude is right, and it's the best, most interesting seed I've got. I'm going to scatter it now, Lord, so here goes. We'll see what comes up in the field."

You'll enjoy his disarming wisdom in the pages of this book as well as *Mastering Contemporary Preaching* and *Hearing God's Voice Above the Noise*.

Knute Larson

Other than the three women in his life — his wife and two daughters — Knute Larson is consumed with twin passions: basketball and ministry.

On one occasion when another editor and I arrived at The Chapel to discuss with him the contents of this book, Knute greeted us with a patch over his right eye.

Waving off our obvious stares, he smiled wryly and said, "I scratched my cornea playing basketball yesterday."

Knute regularly plays lunch-hour pickup games at The Chapel with businessmen from the community — churched and unchurched. His passion for a scrappy game of basketball often leads Knute to his second passion: ministry.

After telling us about a rough-and-tumble basketball game in which he resisted retaliating for or even calling a flagrant foul, Knute said: "Basketball is a contact sport, contrary to what some think. Besides, there are many things more important than calling every foul, like learning self-control and patience while playing.

That's a way I can be a 'light' to those watching me."

Those watching him, besides his basketball teammates, are 6,000 weekend attenders at The Chapel. The Chapel sits on a downtown campus across the street from the University of Akron. The church is widely known for its life-changing ministries to those in pain: the divorced, the addicted, and the bereaved.

Before coming to The Chapel in 1983, Knute, a graduate of Grace Seminary in Winona Lake, Indiana, pastored Grace Brethren Church in Ashland, Ohio, for fifteen years. Of a recent survey of Akron community leaders, Knute was voted among the top fifteen most influential people in the Akron area. He also is the author of *Run Steady, Run Straight*.

Larry Osborne

Larry Osborne didn't have much of a honeymoon.

"Six months into my first senior pastorate, I found myself embroiled in controversy. The church was losing old members as fast as we could bring in new ones. The board and I were having a hard time seeing eye-to-eye on anything. At night, I'd lie in bed and wonder what I'd do if they asked me to leave or the church split or a congregational meeting suddenly turned raucous."

Back then, Larry was determined to make his ministry succeed: "When I arrived at the church, I was armed with books and ideas on growth, evangelism, and reaching the community. If you'd told me to slow down and focus on camaraderie and unity, I'd have chided you for your inward, even self-centered, approach to ministry. We had a world to conquer."

Today, twelve years later, Larry is still at his first senior pastorate, North Coast Church (Evangelical Free) in Vista, California, and now he's determined to help his church develop the very camaraderie and unity he once eschewed: Though his church is thriving (1,600 attenders), he makes small home groups the hub of the ministry. If the percentage of attenders who partake in home groups drops, to say 50 percent, the church stops all efforts at outreach until the numbers in home groups reach 70 percent.

Before coming to North Coast Church, Larry was a youth

pastor in La Crescenta, California. He holds the M.Div and D.Min degrees from Talbot Theological Seminary. He is also author of *The Unity Factor*.

To his understudy, Timothy, the fiery apostle Paul said, "If anyone competes as an athlete, he does not receive the victor's crown unless he competes according to the rules" (2 Tim. 2:5). Timothy had a tough job ahead of him, and Paul wanted to steel him for the hardships endemic to a life of successful leadership.

Our hope is that these three pastors will help you successfully face the enormous challenges of local church ministry.

— *David Goetz*
Assistant editor, LEADERSHIP

Part 1
The Pressures

The heart that recoils in shame over failure to achieve potential tends to swell up with pride over success.
— *Larry Osborne*

CHAPTER ONE

The Burden of Potential

Dave was a gifted leader, though not a great preacher. During his second pastorate, he took a dead, inner-city church and turned it around. Under his guidance the church grew into a vibrant ministry, and attendance soared to over five hundred.

Then a call came from a large suburban church. Many things in him said stay: he was enjoying his ministry, his wife and kids were happy, the church was ecstatic with what Dave was doing. But his drive to be all that he could be in ministry won out. So he went.

The next five years were the worst of his life. He'd gotten in over his head. Of the two skills necessary to succeed in a large church — leadership and a strong pulpit presence — he had only one.

Before long, people began to leave, many of them parting with those famous last words, "I'm not being fed."

Dave was devastated. He'd seldom heard those words before. He'd been more than an adequate communicator in a smaller setting, where people could hear his words and watch his life. But in a setting where people knew only what they heard in the pulpit, he was in trouble.

Today, Dave is out of ministry — a victim of what I've come to call the Potential Trap.

Apparently, Dave is not alone. The results of one survey examining the personal and professional lives of clergy claimed that 50 percent of us feel unable to meet the needs of our jobs, and 70 percent of us say our self-esteem is lower now than when we first entered the ministry.

Something has gone terribly wrong. I don't believe for a moment that God has failed to equip half of us for the tasks he's called us to, or that 70 percent of us need our self-esteem lowered. But I'm not surprised that half of us feel pressured to do more and more, and that 70 percent of us judge ourselves more strictly than even God does.

That's what happens when we unwittingly fall into the trap called Potential.

Be All That You Can Be?

Over the years, the Army has spent a ton of money on advertising because a volunteer army demands recruitment — lots of it. One ad campaign stands out: the series of radio and TV spots imploring listeners to "be all you can be."

These ads play into one of our culture's most deeply held values: maximizing our potential is one of life's greatest responsibilities — anyone who settles for less makes a tragic if not shameful mistake.

That assumption is shared by many of us in ministry. Add to

that the eternal consequences of our work, and no wonder most of us feel driven.

When I arrived at North Coast Church as a rookie pastor, I brought with me a three-ring binder I called my Life Notebook. In it were a series of laminated pages detailing my future dreams. These pages provided me with a concrete picture of what I thought life would look like if and when I reached my fullest potential: I wanted to pastor a church of a thousand or more, to lead a multiple staff, to do outside speaking. It spelled out the location and type of town I hoped to minister in someday. It even contained a detailed description of the house my wife and I wanted — down to its square feet and number of bedrooms.

I referred to that notebook weekly. I used it as a compass. It kept me focused on my goals and insured that the major decisions of my life were moving me in the right direction. It also served as a measuring rod, a standard by which I could judge my progress and realistically discern whether I was a success or failure.

My notebook may have been extreme. But I've found that many of us carry around similar though unwritten expectations within. And we turn to these internal aspirations when we're trying to decide what we are capable of, which challenges to tackle, and how well we are doing in life and ministry.

A number of years ago, however, I began to wonder if something might be wrong. Among other things, I noticed that those of us who were trying to be all that we could be weren't necessarily becoming more Christlike. Instead, we were growing increasingly competitive, self-centered, and dissatisfied.

We were also prone to lose perspective, often feeling like a failure in the midst of success. What lay leader or seminary student wouldn't be honored to lead a Bible study of 120 people? But once a pastor starts focusing on potential, it's easy to complain about having "only" 120 people at a service. Instead of joy over those who are there, we're frustrated by those who don't come.

The pursuit of maximized potential leaves us following a faulty compass, one that always points to the bigger platform, the larger ministry, the more challenging task. It never suggests that we are in over our heads, that the greener grass is only painted, that God might want us to be still rather than charge ahead.

In addition, potential is never reached. There is always something more to do: another mountain to climb, another need to meet, another opportunity I can't afford to miss.

In short, I was setting myself up to feel like a failure. The marvel and joy of being used by God were too easily drowned out by frustration and guilt over all the things yet to be accomplished. Even when I found a way to get it all done, the result was usually a worn out, exhausted pastor hating life and ministry.

I've since analyzed this Potential Trap, and I've discovered some principles that have helped me not only to understand but more importantly to avoid falling back into its jaws.

A Search for Truth

The Potential Trap says we need to exploit fully our gifts and abilities for God. It is, of course, based on the assumption that we can get an accurate read on our gifts and abilities.

But that's a bad assumption.

In spite of, or perhaps to compensate for, our struggles with self-esteem, the vast majority of us rate our relational and leadership skills well above average. One recent *Leadership* survey of pastors found that over 80 percent of us believe we have above-average preaching skills. In a related survey sent to laypeople, over 60 percent of our parishioners said our messages weren't so hot — average or below average!

Obviously, something is out of line. By definition, at least half of us are below average. The problem is, it's always the other guy.

Why do we overrate ourselves?

To begin with, we've all got a sin nature that, as Paul warns in Romans, encourages us to "think more highly of ourselves than we ought to think." In addition, those of us in ministry receive a lot of well-intentioned but frankly deceptive encouragement. If we believe it, we can end up thinking our potential is a lot greater than it really is.

It starts with our first feeble attempts at ministry. As a lay leader, a seminary intern, or first-year assistant, we get a chance to deliver a sermon. As we look back on it years later, most of us think of it as pretty bad. But what do we hear at the door the morning of that first sermon? Nothing but praise. No one is trying to deceive us; it's just their way of encouraging us to keep after it.

Unfortunately, the pattern continues in many churches. Social conventions at the church door call for compliments, not criticisms. Who is going to say, "That was a real dog, Larry. Hope you do better next week"? So Sunday after Sunday, people praise us, even though their words may have little to do with what they think.

All of this has made me slow to accept praise and compliments seriously, especially when they're offered immediately after a sermon. Instead, I've learned to put my stock in what I call second-hand compliments: those things said out of my earshot and without any notion they will be reported back to me.

When someone tells one of our staff members, "Larry's last sermon was perfect for the problem I'm facing now," and it's reported back to me, it means something.

Such realism goes a long way toward avoiding the Potential Trap. It helps me see what gifts I have and just how far I can nurture them — and it's often not as far as my flattered ego thinks.

A Call to Obedience

Growing up in a church, I heard many sermons on Jesus' parable of the talents. The application was always the same: don't waste any of the gifts and talents the Lord has bestowed on you. I took that to mean that the best way to please him and to be obedient to his plan for my life was to make the most out of every opportunity. My goal was to die having gained the greatest return possible with whatever "talents" he gave me.

That's okay as far as it goes. I've since learned, however, that obedience to the Lord sometimes means turning down opportunities. Sometimes it even means intentionally choosing to do or be less than my best in a given situation.

When a seminary president left his post to care for his ailing wife (she had Alzheimer's disease), it created quite a stir. He felt he was faithfully heeding God's call to obedience. But in so doing, let's not forget that he also walked away from a great deal of potential ministry. When he left, he was still capable of accomplishing much that needed to be done. But God wanted him to take care of his wife. So he did.

From time to time, all of us have to work through the same sort of issues. We must never forget that Jesus, in his early thirties — in the prime of ministry, in the prime of life — sacrificed all his talents and ministry opportunities for something greater: obedience to God.

Admittedly, our situations are seldom as dramatic or the price of obedience as costly, but sometimes we have to make the tough choices. If the Master wants me to wash dishes, it doesn't matter if I have the latent skills to be a virtuoso. I belong in the kitchen, not the concert hall.

That doesn't mean turning down every opportunity, but obedience requires careful listening for God's voice. During the middle of my third year here at North Coast, I received a letter from what I considered to be one of the plum churches in our association. They were asking me to apply for the senior pastor position. In fact, it was one of the churches listed on the laminated pages of my Life Notebook as a church I hoped to pastor some day.

At that point, North Coast Church was still fighting through leadership issues. The numbers were small, and growth was stagnant. My self-esteem was taking a beating. Worse, I had little hope that the clouds would break. On the surface the decision looked like a no-brainer: Go for it!

As I read this letter, I was surprised by a sudden and strong sense of God's presence. Before I could even ask, he said, "No." It was more than an inner prompting. It was the clear and unmistakable leading of the Lord.

I was stunned but convinced it was a mystical leading of the Holy Spirit. I wadded the letter, threw it in the trash, and went on with my day.

When those closest to me heard about my decision, most thought I was crazy. Why would I choose to stay in a "dead-end ministry" when a well-known and significantly larger platform was readily available? What a waste of potential!

But that's the point: fulfilling potential and obeying the Lord are not always the same thing.

The Need for Faithfulness

The quest to fulfill self-perceived potential also tends to confuse success with faithfulness.

We all know there's a difference between God's definition of success and the world's. But I've found the more I focus on maximizing my potential, the closer I come to using the world's dictionary instead of God's.

In our culture, fulfilling potential has more to do with tangible results than how the game is played. When we contemplate fulfilling our potential, we seldom think about martyrdom. We're not even thinking about faithfully toiling away in relative obscurity. We're thinking about winning, overcoming obstacles, numbers, success.

Driven people are seldom driven to be good. They are driven to win. That's true of even ministers. We set our sights on being successful — larger attendance, larger staff, larger budget — often on the assumption that being successful and faithful are one and the same.

During my early years here at North Coast, I took failures hard. Whether we were struggling with a lack of unity, lackluster worship, or stagnant growth, I assumed the blame, sure that God was sorely disappointed with me. I strove to get my act together, pray more, study more, sin less, increase my faith and vision — hoping then things would turn around.

The result was a lot of sleepless nights, a battered sense of self-worth, and a joyless ministry.

Then one day I came across a passage in Proverbs that became a catalyst for a radical change in my outlook: "There is no wisdom, no insight, no plan that can succeed against the Lord. The horse is made ready for the day of battle, but victory rests with the Lord" (Prov. 21:30–31).

The key insight was this: I wasn't ultimately responsible for success or failure. Though I'd read it many times before, I'd never actually applied this verse to my ministry. While I could certainly sabotage my ministry, thereby guaranteeing failure, there was nothing I could do to guarantee victory. That was out of my control. My job was simply to prepare the horse for battle the best I could. It was God's job to decide who won and who lost the battle.

This revolutionary insight called for a drastic change in the goals I set and the way I judged my ministry. I had to stop asking how successful or unsuccessful our church was and start asking how faithfully I was preparing it for battle.

Among other things, that meant shifting from a focus on numerical growth to spiritual health. For example, home fellowship groups are key to our discipleship emphasis. We want to have 70 percent of our Sunday morning attenders involved in them. So now, whenever the percentage drops below that, we stop all communication with visitors — something we've done twice. We get tough, because we do not want to grow faster than we can assimilate people. The goal is a horse better prepared for the battle: not more people attending North Coast but more people growing in the Lord and doing ministry.

Furthermore, this insight helped me accept some failures and not wallow in self-criticism. For example, while we minister to singles through our home fellowship groups, so far we've been unable to put together a successful singles ministry — this despite the fact that singles make up a major portion of our community and church. We've tried a couple of programs to draw them out, but the programs failed.

I'm concerned about that, but today I don't take it as a major blow to my ego. I've found that I can suffer a defeat I've done nothing to create. Not that I've became a fatalist. I still work hard to win. I still plan strategically. I still hate to lose. But I no longer equate a rough road or even an outright failure as a spiritual problem on my part.

A Different Ministry

Ironically, our decision to focus on health has fueled growth. Maybe it's not so ironic: once I gave up the manipulation of numbers and concentrated on ministry to people, it's only natural more people were interested in coming. Perhaps being faithful has something to do with one of the great spiritual mysteries: we gain life by losing it, and we enhance ministry by giving up the yearning for successful ministry.

Still, I mention this growth with some hesitancy. I do not for a second believe that the formula for growth is to relinquish the pursuit of potential, concentrating on spiritual health. I shifted my focus when our attendance hung around 150, and stayed with that focus as it continued to hover at that figure for a couple of years more. I had no idea that the church would grow, and that was okay. I had already begun releasing myself from the Potential Trap. The joy and fulfillment of ministry had already returned.

I can't say I'm completely free of the Potential Trap; with the opportunities that come with a larger church, I'm still tempted to fall back into it. I still live in a culture that harangues me to become self-actualized. A large part of me is still driven. But I've discovered that the heart that recoils in shame over failure to achieve potential tends to swell up with pride over success. I don't want that kind of heart, nor do I want to fall back into the trap called potential. Ministry is too great a privilege not to enjoy.

Our reputation must begin from the inside out.
— Knute Larson

CHAPTER TWO

In Need of a Good Reputation

I sat in the waiting area of a car wash, reading a newspaper, waiting for my car to move through the automated wash. Glancing sideways, I saw a pair of female legs in Bermuda shorts. I fought the urge to take a second look and buried my face in the newspaper. The woman stopped and dropped into the seat next to me.

"Well, did you run this morning?" she asked.

Surprised, I looked over. "Yes, I did." I didn't recognize her. "How did you know I run?"

"I attend the early service at The Chapel, and a couple of times you've mentioned your running."

After she left, I shuddered at what might have been: had I taken a double-take at her legs and then met her eyes — that would have been a dumb misstep on my part.

I recently read a comment by an NBA star who, when asked about the effect his immoral off-the-court behavior had on young admirers, said, "Hey, I didn't ask to be a role model." In one sense, we pastors *have* asked to be role models. How we act outside the church's walls impacts our work as much as how we act inside them.

Maybe more! High visibility adds an extra pressure never to drop my guard, never to give in to temptation. God writes a strong standard for pastors in 1 Timothy 3, making the consequences of a pastor's public failure even more painful. We never exit the public stage. While God looks on the heart and not on outward appearances, the people we lead and the community in which we serve have only our outward actions to gauge our character.

Reputation Tested

Living in this glass house is, however, only one aspect of the reputation pressures we face. Those pressures come in various settings and can either strengthen us or make us want to run.

● *In intimate groups.* I've met with a pastor friend regularly for over twenty-four years. We enjoy each other's loyalty and talk about everything from our personal finances to our sex lives. Nothing we say is off limits; we're never shocked at each other's honesty.

But it's a struggle to know how transparent to be with church members, even church leaders. When people in small group Bible studies take turns sharing their struggles, I can't reveal just anything. If I was totally honest about every whim or thought, I would lose their respect: most people don't really want to know that their pastor struggles with certain issues. At the same time, however, I like to relax and not pretend. I do want to lead by example. But by revealing too much, we can hobble our reputations, crippling our ability to effectively lead.

● *When things aren't going well.* During my first five years of ministry at The Chapel, 300 to 500 people (about 10 percent of the church) left for "greener" pastures. Most of their reasons for leaving could be traced to me. They simply didn't like me or the changes my arrival brought, or they believed rumors about supposed changes.

Few things are more threatening to a pastor than to have people leave the church. It makes some people question your effectiveness, and it tempts you either to act defensively or to blame yourself.

● *When confidentiality is the issue.* Once I had to release a staff member for breaking a clear staff policy and for refusing to stop. That was painful. And I chose to protect him and his family by not announcing the reason.

Tragically, a few weeks later, this man committed suicide. When the word got out that I had just let him go, some members wondered if my treatment had pushed him over the brink. They shared it liberally.

Later, while I was talking to some businessmen in a downtown hotel lobby, a man shouted across the lobby, "You killed Bill, and now you're trying to kill Tony!" (alluding to another staff conflict). Still, I chose to maintain confidentiality and refused to divulge all that had gone on with the former staff member.

In certain circumstances, when we can't or choose not to divulge confidential information, people will question our reputations. (What was it that Truman said about heat in the kitchen?)

● *When you strive for excellence.* Ironically, when we're really concerned about the success of the church, it can inadvertently threaten our reputations.

Early in my ministry here at The Chapel, I probably wrote too many staff policies for too many things. I believed policies should not exist unless they were written and unambiguous. Things like office dress, weekly reports, moral code, unity goals, and definitions of acceptable conference or study leave — all these were put on paper. Much to the sorrow of some who work around me, I love charts and goals and reports.

So I wrote lots of memos, and we went over them in staff meetings. That seemed much more efficient to me than telling people these things face to face, one by one. I liked results, worked long hours, and expected the same from those I led.

To some of the staff, though, my drivenness for excellence came across as legalistic, impersonal, and oppressive. Since then, I've learned how to make changes more slowly and gracefully, caring more for people along the way.

I still bristle a little when I think about how "right" I was. I was the senior staff member, and policies do need to be clear and on paper. The "Aw, shucks" method does not work after the church grows to a certain size. But being right is not the only concern, especially when leading a team. Being careful is important. Taking your time is essential. Building relationships is primary. Then you write the policies together!

● *At significant junctures.* When I arrived at The Chapel, I wrestled with creating a larger vision for the church. I felt The Chapel's large Sunday-morning gathering needed to be supplemented by medium-sized groups (40 to 80 people), to allow for relationships, pastoral care, and nurture.

When I began to try to enact this vision, I encountered opposition, and some of it came from the staff. I then realized how much was at stake. I was essentially hazarding my professional reputation on this new vision: if it failed, I failed.

Two years passed before even some of the staff got behind the vision. It was a long two years.

From the Inside Out

The French have a phrase, *déformation professionnelle*, which means "the unraveling of one's job." The idea is that over time it's easy to stop enjoying your job, to do it with your hands but not your heart. A quarterback who has lost his desire to win, for example, is more apt to make mental mistakes, which sabotage his play and ensure that he won't win.

The danger is extreme for pastors. So, monitoring our inner lives is critical. Having a reputation for being a caring and faithful pastor starts with being a caring and faithful person, inside. For me that amounts to two things.

● *Stay close to Christ.* During John Sununu's tenure as President Bush's chief of staff, I read an article in *Time* magazine describing Sununu as a "tiger in the White House."

A reporter had asked, "Isn't your job difficult?"

"No," Sununu replied.

The reporter, thinking Sununu hadn't understood his question, repeated it. Sununu replied, "No, my job isn't difficult. I have only one constituent" — who, of course, was President Bush.

Ultimately, we too have only one constituent: Jesus Christ. Our relationship with him matters most. A growing, true, personal spiritual life with Christ is the cornerstone of building a public reputation. For me, that has meant, among other things, more self-control.

One of my passions is basketball, and twice a week I play pickup games in our church gym during lunch with a group of local businessmen. One of the rules is that the person who fouls calls the foul.

Once I was hammered hard while moving to my right for what would have been a great jump shot. One of my teammates started arguing with the guy who fouled me, saying, "You fouled Knute. You've got to call it!" The man who had fouled me didn't reply. I decided not to say anything and continued play, heading for the other end of the floor.

After the game, this teammate, a high-powered lawyer, said, "Didn't he foul you, Knute?"

"Yes," I replied, "but you call your own fouls."

Later, before leaving the locker room, this man stopped by and smiled, "You know, Knute, I've got to learn to have patience like you do."

Basketball is a "contact sport," contrary to what some think, but there are many things more important than correctly calling fouls: learning self-control and patience while playing, plus being a "light" to those who are watching you.

● *Stay close to home.* One of the nicest comments I've received came from one of my daughters: "You're no different at home than you are at church, and we like that." That meant a lot to me because it showed some integrity: who I was in my private world was consistent with the image I projected in public. That is a continuing goal.

But it's never been easy. Nineteen years ago my wife hit me over the head with a two-by-eight when she said, "Knute, I think you're doing a great job with the church, but I don't think I know you."

Ever since, we've gone out to breakfast most Thursdays and created a master schedule to monitor my time. I've also scheduled individual appointments with our two girls each week and tried to reserve Monday and Friday evenings for the entire family. It was the best way I could keep balance in my life and take my focus off of work, from which I draw immense satisfaction and energy.

External Impressions to Foster

After a friend of mine found out I had accepted the call to The Chapel, he phoned, saying, "Good luck on your suicide mission." He had heard about the distinguished ministry of my predecessor, who had pastored there for twenty-five years, and his father, who had founded the church and ministered there twenty-five years previous to his son. Both were effective, successful leaders. My well-wisher thought my ministry would be only an "unintentional interim." Ugh.

Ten years have passed, and I've discovered that this man's death wish contained partial truth the first few years. Those transition days, good as they were in public, had me working with a staff I did not choose and who did not choose me (a few were very clear about that). I also grappled with the "good ghosts" of the past, which are sometimes worse than following "bad skeletons"!

My friend-adviser Lyle Schaller had told me on the phone, "Brace yourself, honor the past, be yourself, and do what's right. The first years may feel unfair, but then it will get better."

He was right. Whether making a single change or striving for a successful ministry, I've got to demonstrate that I am a trustworthy person. In that regard, there are many things to consider.

● *Work hard.* Not long ago, in a Bible study I was attending with younger men — men in their thirties and forties — a well-respected older gentleman remarked, "You guys work too hard. You ought to stop worrying about your reputation and how hard you work; turn your business over to God."

I couldn't resist objecting: "But Dutch, could you have done that before you were sixty? Do you think any of these guys can do it in their thirties?" Part of the drivenness in our early years, I believe, is positive. We can't expect to be successful — can't expect to be respected by our congregations — if we haven't paid our dues. And one of those dues is hard work.

● *Work smart.* Many corporate business leaders attend our church and understand the challenge of leading a church as large as The Chapel. They expect not only that I work hard but that I wisely use my time.

I frequently get input from these business and spiritual leaders. I meet with three small groups of men, have breakfast and lunch appointments almost every weekday, and use advisers regularly. I try to ensure my time is well-utilized.

● *Don't answer the unanswerable.* Shortly after my sister's death at age 14, a woman said to my mother, "Your daughter's death was for a purpose. Maybe she would have grown up to be a prostitute."

This person's insensitivity was the result of her feeling compelled to give an answer for everything. I think that admitting we don't know the reason for this baby's death or that person's cancer is often difficult, but to do otherwise makes us appear indifferent to people's suffering.

One of my favorite cartoons is of a man standing on a mountain and speaking to God, saying, "Tell me why."

The voice out of heaven replies, "Okay, I'll tell you why."

The man, cheered by this response, awaits eagerly for the divine reason, but the answer he gets from God is, "Just because."

Just because — sometimes there are no explainable reasons. Often the only thing our people need to see from us is our humanness, our limited and broken understanding. By confessing our ignorance of God's ways, we can actually lend credibility to our ministry.

● *Care for the community.* On Wednesday evenings, I work through supper and often make a window stop at McDonald's for a chicken fajita. I've gotten to know an employee who's been working each Wednesday I stop there.

During that quick stop, I've learned about her recent hospital stay, her poor family, her concerns about her future, her ulcers. I've told her I would pray for her. Only recently has she found out that I'm a pastor at The Chapel.

My goal is to reach out to everyone I brush up against in the community. I want to get to know the city. I attend cocktail parties (though I sip only diet cola), pray at public events, and, when asked, lead devotions for the local professional sports teams.

● *Be professional.* If you asked several of my staff members about my desire to dress right, they'd probably quip, "Knute only loosens his tie when he goes to bed at night." I say I'm tempted to mow my lawn with my tie on just in case someone from the church drives by.

Like it or not, though, dressing impacts how we're perceived. By our appearance, we project an image about our competence. In the culture where The Chapel is located, professionals dress in suit and tie, so I've made wearing a tie to the office a standard for all of our staff. Outside of the office, I expect them to dress appropriate to the occasion.

● *Demonstrate love.* Whether conscious or not, people want leaders who know where they are going and who love people. In writing about the love pastors need to show their people, many have noted the importance of "perceived love" — public actions that symbolize love to the congregation. On the surface, perceived love sounds hypocritical, but the point is that we must overtly make sure those we love know we love them. I do this differently with the different groups in the church.

1. Lay leaders and staff. Besides learning to communicate more personally with staff, I've also painfully learned the art of disagreement. At first I náively thought that because I desired open

and honest disagreement in meetings, staff members and lay leaders would feel free to air their concerns. Therefore I assumed silence meant consent. I was wrong.

Often the staff would nod in apparent agreement. Later, however, I would sometimes discover their disagreements through other sources. Perhaps my reactions or defensiveness in staff meetings showed too much, discouraging free discussion. Today I encourage a variety of opinions, wait more patiently for all sides to speak up, and thank people for healthy give and take.

I work hard at being open and human, and I'm "Knute" with the staff and leaders I work with. It's not that hard to say, "I don't know," anymore or even, "I love you and appreciate your honesty" (or "insight" or "enthusiasm" or whatever).

2. The congregation. I grew up in a divorced home and, though my parents loved me, I never heard them say to me, "I love you" until I was an adult.

Around his fiftieth year, my father began telling me he loved me, but only after I would say, "I love you," first. About a year ago, at age 76, my father died of a sudden heart attack on Father's Day. The night prior to his death, I had called him, and before we hung up, for the first time he was the first to say, "I love you." He wasn't aware of my tears, but I sensed he could feel my joy.

Consequently, I've made it a point with those I love to say, "I love you," though it doesn't come naturally for me. I even do this regularly with my congregation, saying, "I just want to remind you how much you all mean to me and the staff. I love you."

Guarding Your Reputation

Only one serious misstep is needed to damage what has taken years to create. Here are four areas I monitor to ensure my reputation is always above board.

1. *The opposite sex.* One time a woman in the church wanted to thank me for the help I'd given to a local ministry in Akron.

"May I give you a hug before I leave?" she asked.

"Sure," I said. I then called my secretary into my office and said, "This woman would like to give me a hug. Come on in." A polite hug followed.

Several staff guidelines monitor relationships with the opposite sex. No staff member, for example, is permitted to meet alone with the opposite sex. Nor is any staff member permitted to be alone in a car with someone other than his or her spouse. Nor can staff members do sustained counseling with members of the opposite sex.

The best defense is a good offense. We'd rather aggressively seek out ways to stave off potential temptations than to deal with the aftermath of rumors or a fallen comrade.

Obviously, only I can guard my heart and thoughts. Any of us could lie to our accountability groups. My friend Jerry asks, "How's your sex life?" or "Are you praying?" — and I ask him the same and harder. But we must stay with the truth and guard our own spirits. "Take heed to your spirit," Malachi said.

2. The tongue. I shifted back and forth as I waited impatiently in the checkout line. I was becoming increasingly annoyed. I was in a hurry, and the woman in front of me acted as if she had all day to pay for her parcels. Leisurely she made small talk with the cashier — something about her kids' plans for the summer. Inside I groaned, *Why does this always happen to me?*

When she finally headed for the door, I slid my items in front of the cashier. I felt like saying something sarcastic, to show the cashier my irritation. But I held my tongue, smiled, and, when my groceries were totaled, wrote a check for the amount.

"Oh, Knute Larson!" gushed the cashier after she looked at my check. "I listen to you on the radio every day. You've really helped me."

"Uh, thank you," I mumbled. I grabbed my grocery bags and stumbled out of the store, thanking the Lord for the good sense not to spout off to this cashier.

I don't think I've ever gotten used to the fact that my words are often public domain. I sometimes feel my ministry is always a comment away from disaster.

3. Money. I've made a conscious attempt to distance myself from money. As with the opposite sex, the best offense is good defense. So I never handle church money. Period. If someone tries to hand me an offering envelope, I don't accept it; I direct the giver to one of our ushers or financial deacons.

4. *Opponents.* Even after carefully building and guarding our reputations, sometimes the pastor's name will be unfairly dragged through the mud. I heard about one pastor who, after a false accusation of sexual abuse, was forced to leave his church.

I've felt such attacks myself. A woman who, before her conversion, participated in a satanic cult, told me she and her fellow Satan worshipers had prayed that I would fall morally. Needless to say, such incidents frighten me, so prayer about such matters is a regular part of staff prayer times.

Aside from prayer, there is not much we can do to squelch rumors. When I've heard rumors circulating about certain actions I've taken, occasionally I've taken aside the leaders and staff and said, "You may hear such and such, but this is the truth."

Obviously, I believe there is no sense addressing such things in worship services and spreading the rumors further!

All in all, I resist answering my critics. No need to return evil for evil. I want to be known as someone who can handle pressure and pain. At some point, when we're under fire, the only thing we can do is go home each evening, go to bed, and trust that, given enough time, the truth will win out.

Honor from Above

Through the years, I've learned that what some people think really doesn't matter. On one occasion, when my wife and I were having a late breakfast at a local restaurant on a Thursday morning, a man from our church stopped at our table, looked at his watch, and said, "Having breakfast at 10:15. Must be nice."

Earlier that morning — 1:30 A.M. — I had been called to the hospital because of a car accident. Still I had made it to my 6:30 A.M. radio program and taken my children to school.

Resisting my first thought, to toss my hot tea at him, I said with a smile, "Yes, it really is nice."

No matter what your reputation, you can't please everyone. But the positives of being "on stage," for me, have always outweighed the negatives. The greatest reward, however, will come at the finish line with our Savior. To those who run his way, he will say, "Well done, my good and faithful servant."

Ministry is often a string of cramped positions, where problems and limitations are just disguised opportunities for ministering in new and creative ways.

— *Larry Osborne*

CHAPTER THREE
Ministry from a Cramped Position

When I first came to North Coast, the walls of the "sanctuary" were not lined with stained glass. They were spotted with the remains of innumerable food fights. While we rented the facility on Sundays, Monday through Friday it served another function: lunchroom for the local high school.

Obviously, it wasn't an ambiance that lent itself to traditional worship. One Sunday a dog wandered up the aisle in the middle of my sermon, nuzzling and sniffing at the faithful. Another Sunday, a boisterous gang of adolescent skateboarders decided to show off their skills right outside a row of large Plexiglas windows.

On top of that, I had taken a cut in pay from my previous salary as a youth pastor in a large suburban church. As the new pastor of a fledgling church plant, I no longer had at my disposal a secretary, copy machine, or many of the other trappings of civilized ministry. Instead, my new office was a refurbished garage with a beat-up desk that my previous church had given me as an act of charity.

After a quick start (we jumped from 120 to 150 in a few weeks), we leveled off. It soon became obvious that ministry from a cramped position would not be a short-term aberration but a long-term way of life.

As a 28-year-old rookie pastor, I had two choices: adjust or quit. I chose to adjust, all the time thinking that if I hung in there long enough, the day would finally come when ministry from a cramped position with significantly limited resources would be a thing of the past.

That day never came. I've since discovered that there is no time in ministry when something doesn't hinder ministry. Today we have more staff and volunteers, and larger facilities than I ever imagined, yet I still often feel cramped. We always need more space, money, and workers to do ministry right.

Being cramped, then, seems to be a part of ministry at every turn, at every level of growth — and probably at every church. We have no choice: if we are going to minister, we're going to have to learn how to do it from a cramped position.

Here are some things that have helped our church succeed in less-than-ideal circumstances.

Ignore Some Cramps

Pastors commonly — and mistakenly — assume that if something is wrong, we have to fix it. Whether the pressure comes from well-meaning and caring members or from our sense of duty, I've learned that, in many cases, it's a good idea to ignore those pressures and let the problem be.

Yet one of the hardest facts to accept when ministering from a cramped position is that you're not going to have a well-balanced ministry. When you're working under severe budgetary constraints, for example, shoring up one program inevitably means taking away from another.

During a critical stage of our church's growth, we had a lot of young families with small children, and we had some older adults. But we had almost no families with junior high or high school kids. So we poured our limited resources into creating a top-notch children's program. As a result, we attracted more people with young children. But we had a huge demographic gap where youth ministry was supposed to exist.

Still, there were a few families with junior and senior high kids. It was hard to look them in the eye and say, "I'm sorry, but we just can't minister to your kids right now." But that's exactly what I had to say to one man I dearly love, the father of two high school girls. He understood our limitations and continued to support me and the church, and he's one of our elders today. But it was hard for him —and for me — to ignore this area of weakness in our program.

Of course, it's a lot easier to ignore those pressures if we offer the congregation a compelling alternative. Peter Drucker calls it building on our islands of strength — which we did by focusing on families with young children.

That's why, when we hired our first full-time staff person, we resisted the powerful temptation to make youth work part of his job description. I went to the board and asked them to make a rule that Mike would not work with youth. I wanted the church officially to declare that we were going to ignore this area of weakness and focus on building our strengths, which at that time were our children's ministry and home groups. The board agreed. Eventually, those islands became so strong and brought in enough new people and new funding that we were able to develop an outstanding youth program. But the key was waiting until the time was ripe rather than trying to fix it at the first sign of brokenness.

This principle continues to guide us today. Right now, for example, our missions effort is anemic at best. Because our church has been growing rapidly, we've put a lot of effort into absorbing and ministering to new people. So our missions emphasis has taken a back seat.

Does this mean that we don't care about the Great Commission? Of course not. We were active in missions during the years when growth was stagnant. I'm confident we'll be a missions church again in the future. But right now, we're expanding the kingdom by focusing on that corner of the kingdom that is bulging our own walls.

"Be what you are — don't try to be what you are not" is a slogan that helps me work effectively within limitations.

Bend with the Church's Attitude

Before coming to North Coast, all the churches I had worked in had been large churches, where the unspoken questions are about quality: Are things done with excellence? Is the preaching powerful? Is the music polished and professional?

But the unspoken questions in a small church are different. Lyle Schaller suggests there are only three:

1. Do you love me?
2. Do you love me?
3. Do you *really* love me?

In a small church, few care if Aunt Martha's solo is a little off-key; that's Aunt Martha; everybody knows and loves her. But in a large church, everyone squirms if Aunt Martha misses a note. To my harm, I came into the little church and looked and listened with big-church eyes and ears. I focused on excellence and performance. I even canned our Aunt Martha.

If that wasn't insensitive enough, I made a similar mistake with the woman in charge of our newsletter. I was troubled with our newsletter's jokes, puns, and in-house references, like, "The Blond Bomber hit a home run at the church picnic." I thought newcomers reading the newsletter would feel left out. To me, a newsletter should be a vehicle for communicating with those on the inside *and* the fringe of our ministry.

So I sat down with the woman who put it together and explained my concerns. I said it as gently as I knew how, but all I succeeded in doing was crushing her feelings. Three weeks later, she and her family left the church.

Regardless of the size of the church, though, there is often a basic attitude difference between pastor and people that we must recognize and accept. The pastor's mindset is visionary; he or she sees the future potential and envisions what the church can become. But the mindset of the congregation is more often static: people have come because they like what the church is. Their vision of the future is "More of the same, please."

I've learned, then, simply to accept these differences in perspective and be more pastoral about any changes I make or challenges I present.

Give Volunteers a Break

Since I was the church's only paid employee, and there was no funding for support staff, I had to rely heavily upon volunteers.

In the beginning, I was frustrated. I had previously relied on an efficient secretarial pool. Volunteers were well-intentioned but often inconsistent, inefficient, and unreliable. They didn't do things the way I wanted them done.

But I've learned how to work from this cramped position. First, I've changed my attitude. I now realize that while a church ministry is my life and my career, it is only a side dish on the volunteer's plate. A volunteer can and will call in sick at the last moment when a paid staff person might drag him- or herself to work. That's a pain. But the truth is, many times I would love to do the same but don't only because I'm paid to be there.

Still, volunteers are fabulous, dedicated, committed people. In addition to the demands of their jobs and families, they give hours of time and energy to keep the ministry of our church humming. To begrudge their inherent limitations is to miss out on one of God's special blessings.

Second, I make sure they're given the best tools to do their jobs. Good volunteers may save the church money, but keeping them isn't cheap.

I once observed our volunteers folding bulletins and newsletters by hand, and I thought to myself, *This is boring, lousy, grunt work. If these people are going to volunteer their time, they deserve to have the job made as easy as possible.* So even though our church was still small and struggling, we bought the best folding machine available. It's a pattern we follow today. No matter how tight the budget, we try to ensure that our volunteers have reliable copy machines, efficient computers, and trustworthy printers. Quality tools make a big difference in morale and in ministry.

Third, we've taken the pressure off some of our volunteers by making the job as manageable as possible. For instance, we found that our volunteer Sunday school teachers were often ill-prepared when they stepped into the classroom. You know the routine: sometime late Saturday night, the teacher cracks the David C. Cook lesson book for the first time and ends up reading or stumbling through the lesson on Sunday morning.

There's an old rule of thumb in business: if three people in a row fail at the same job, the problem is not the people; it's the job. In a similar vein, if volunteer after volunteer comes to class underprepared, perhaps the job needs to be redefined.

That's what we did. We got rid of the traditional teacher and class setup and replaced them with storytellers and shepherds, and we began a program called, "Kids' Praise." We brought all the kids together for a fast-moving, entertaining, Sesame Street-type program led by a good storyteller. (We've found it's a lot easier to find four or five good storytellers than to recruit eighteen Sunday school teachers.)

These leaders conduct a program of music, humor, and fun; the gathering then breaks into small groups. An adult "shepherd" leads each group of children through a simple, loosely structured craft and discussion time. There's no lesson to teach, nothing to prepare for. While they lead the children in a craft, the shepherds encourage the kids to talk about the lesson presented in the larger group. Their function is not to teach but to be a loving, adult presence — a much easier job description for volunteers.

Look for Partners, Not Helpers

As the church grew, we reached a point where we needed to add support staff. There was enough money to hire a part-time secretary and a part-time ministry assistant. Naturally, I felt I needed a full-time person at each position!

At first, I decided to lessen my load by hiring a part-time assistant to do all the things I hated doing. But before long the relationship soured, and I had to let him go.

Back to cramped square one. This time, though, I took a fresh approach: I decided to ignore my needs for support staff and hire ministry staff.

I pooled the money that would have been spent on a part-time secretary and part-time assistant and hired a full-time associate pastor. Instead of being hired to do what I didn't want to do, he was hired to do what I couldn't do. He brought a set of ministry gifts and skills that complemented mine. My overall workload wasn't reduced, but our ministry was multiplied. He's still with us years later, and he now shares the preaching load. But in those early years, it meant I didn't have a secretary. Still we were capable of doing a lot more for the kingdom.

Frankly, sometimes I found it hard to share ministry with a partner. To have a secretary or ministry assistant would have sometimes been easier on my self-esteem, like the first time someone in our church asked Mike to perform a baptism. Until then, I had done all the baptisms, so Mike told this person, "I'm sure it will be no problem, but let me check with Larry."

He came into my office and asked me about it. I had somewhat of a relationship with the person being baptized, and I remember wondering why this person chose Mike over me. But I said, "Sure, go ahead."

After Mike walked out, another associate, Paul, whom we had later hired, stepped into my office and closed the door. He had overheard the conversation. "That was tough, wasn't it?" he said. "How do you feel?"

"Not so great," I said.

That conversation gave me helpful insights into myself. Yes, it did hurt a little. I should have been happy that someone asked Mike to do this baptism. My goal, after all, was to create a shared ministry. In the long run, such discomfort is worth it.

Improve It

No matter how many ways you adapt a building, it always seems to prove inadequate in one way or another. Figuring out how to minister in a less-than-ideal facility is one of the most challenging aspects of ministry.

A year after I arrived, we moved out of our elegant cafeteria with its spaghetti-bedecked walls, and we rented space in a church that held its meetings on Saturdays. Though it was a definite step up, we still had plenty to complain about: the lighting was terrible, the sound system inadequate, and we were still squeezed for classroom space. Furthermore, we felt stymied by being renters, not owners. Cramped again.

The temptation was to crank up a building fund to escape, but that would have taken years to accumulate. And the financial drain would have stifled our fledgling ministry.

Then it dawned on us: why not offer to improve the facility at our expense? Our landlords were pleased to let us invest in their facility, so we fixed the lighting, improved the sound system, and even paid half the expense of a building-expansion program. We couldn't fix our problem, but we sure could improve upon what we had.

As our congregation continued to grow, we ran into a new problem. Our landlords decided we were getting too big for their facility, and they informed us that they were breaking our lease — without notice. In effect, they were kicking a church of eight hundred out in the street!

We could have sued and forced the church to honor the remaining four years of the lease, but we felt it would be unbiblical to take another church to court — and it would have given the local press a religious scandal to run with. So we decided to pack our bags and go.

Our congregation was too large to move into a storefront, we didn't have enough time or money to put up a building, and no other church properties were available. But by God's providence, we found a large building in an industrial complex. It was a retail frontage, with a warehouse and loading docks in the back. It had plenty of parking. And it was the only place in the area that was large enough to permit us to grow.

But many hearts sank when folks first saw their new "church" — half the floor was at ground level, and the other half five feet lower running back to the loading dock. It made some long for the good old days in the cafeteria!

Again we were forced to find a way to improve what we couldn't fix. We angled the cement drop-off and created a ramped floor, which gave us a creative and functional sanctuary space. Ours may be the only retail-space church in America with such a fabulously sloped floor!

Make Lemonade

Cramped quarters can also make discipleship a challenge. All along we've had trouble getting adequate classroom space, especially for adults. Not having adequate facilities for formal or large gatherings can lead to one of two things: you can complain about what isn't or make creative use of what is. We've chosen the latter. If we couldn't meet in Sunday school classes on Sunday morning, we could at least meet in small groups in homes in the evenings.

As a result, home fellowship groups have become the hub of our ministry (and ironically, the most significant contributor to the health of our church). Today over 70 percent of our Sunday morning worshipers attend one of these groups. They study in greater depth the Scripture passage preached on Sunday, giving everyone a common focus and allowing people to deepen their knowledge of Scripture and relationships with one another.

This is perhaps the best lemonade we've made from the lemons we've been handed. We wouldn't go back to adult Sunday school classes even if we had the space to do so.

That's Ministry

As I write this, the 1980s are commonly being viewed as the decade of consumption and the 1990s as the decade of limits. It may well be that a lot of pastors and churches will have to learn to live within their limitations and find creative ways to minister from a cramped position.

Does that mean we have to trim our idealism and vision for the future? Must we downsize our goal of expanding the kingdom of God? Absolutely not! Limitations don't have to diminish our effectiveness. Limitations just force us to be more creative as God expands his kingdom.

Looking back, I believe my greatest mistake when first confronted with cramped quarters was comparing my situation with others. I began feeling I couldn't do anything because I lacked the resources others had. I periodically slumped into a mood of paralysis and defeat.

But no more. I now look at limitations from a new perspective, tinker with solutions, and try to come up with the most enterprising and inventive answers I can. Our church is not something we've planned or engineered. It has evolved as we've looked for creative solutions to our cramped circumstances.

In fact, I've come to believe that restricted ministry is in some ways part and parcel of ministry: it's a string of cramped positions, where problems and limitations are just disguised opportunities for ministering in new and creative ways.

I know I can get a quick response if I preach to felt needs,
but that doesn't mean I've preached successfully.
— *Stuart Briscoe*

CHAPTER FOUR

What Is Successful Preaching?

Many years ago, during the cold war, I traveled to Poland for several weeks of itinerant ministry. One winter day my sponsors drove me in the dead of night to the middle of nowhere. I walked into a dilapidated building crammed with one hundred young people. I realized this was a unique opportunity.

Through an interpreter I preached from John 15 on "Abiding in Christ." Ten minutes into my message, the lights went out. Pitch black.

My interpreter urged me to keep talking. Unable to see my

notes or read my Bible, I continued. After I had preached in the dark for twenty minutes, the lights suddenly blinked on, and what I saw startled me: everyone was on their knees, and they remained there for the rest of my message.

The next day I commented on this to one man, and he said, "After you left, we stayed on our knees most of the night. Your teaching was new to us. We wanted to make sure we were abiding in Christ."

Nights like that make you want to keep preaching!

It usually isn't that easy to know whether preaching has been a "success." Most of us preach each week to largely the same people, people accustomed to our speaking rhythms and themes, who perhaps take us for granted. Our people rarely tell us more than "I enjoyed the sermon, Pastor."

But like any worker, we need to know if our aim is accurate, if our preaching is accomplishing its purpose.

We not only need it, most of us want this information. After shooting an arrow, we run to the target to see if we've hit the bull's eye. We cherish any objective measure of results: letters of appreciation, people coming forward after the sermon, extraordinary comments afterward.

A Tricky Business

Objective feedback, though needed, is unreliable. If I judged the success of my preaching by the standard of my night in Poland, I would be mostly disappointed. We rarely see our listeners so visibly moved.

Furthermore, most pastors who complete an annual denominational report sense the discrepancy between what numbers say about a church and what God is doing in people's lives.

The question of whether our preaching has succeeded is clouded by many factors.

• *Who's evaluating?* Recently I preached a sermon on work. Conscious that a number of people in the congregation were out of work, I mentioned they should not feel useless. "While you get your unemployment benefits, you could work at church doing something significant."

After the service a number of people thanked me for being sensitive to their situation and said they would like to be given something to do at church. But one woman objected to my "socialist attitudes." She said she knew I was British, and Britain was socialist (Maggie Thatcher would have been surprised!). "You have no business dragging socialism into the American church!"

What scores 9.9 with one person, in one tradition, in one part of the country, in one church may take a nose dive elsewhere.

Individual needs also skew a listener's opinion. If a woman, devastated over her crumbling marriage, hears a sermon on "Why Be Committed to the Local Church," she may consider the sermon self-serving propaganda. If the preacher happens to talk about "What to Do When Your Marriage Is Falling Apart," she'll regard it as the greatest thing since the Sermon on the Mount.

If we look at success from God's point of view, some of the greatest sermons ever preached, by the prophets for example, have received a thumbs-down from the congregation. So who listens and how they listen makes a huge difference.

● *What is good?* After one sermon, a woman shook the pastor's hand at the door and went on and on: "That sermon was one of the most wonderful I've ever heard!"

The pastor, being necessarily humble, said, "Oh it really wasn't me. It was all the Lord."

"Oh no," she replied, "It wasn't that good."

It's hard to know what people mean when they tell us about our preaching. Getting a "Not bad" from a hyper-critical person may mean "Wonderful!" From a tactful diplomat it may mean "Horrible!"

● *The seen and unseen.* I preached at a chapel service at Trinity Evangelical Divinity School in Deerfield, Illinois, and afterward a man with a European accent introduced himself to me. "I've been looking forward to seeing you again," he said.

"When did we last meet?" I asked.

"Twenty-five years ago, I was a student in the Bible college where you taught the Book of Romans. Ever since, I've wanted to tell you how much that meant to me. The Book of Romans changed my life. In fact, I now teach Romans at a church in my native Slovakia."

"Are you a pastor?" I asked.

"No."

The man's friend, standing beside him, interjected, "He is a leading nuclear physicist in Eastern Europe."

I ministered in Indonesia recently, and a woman who runs an orphanage in Java said to me, "I should have written you long before, but I just want to tell you how much your preaching meant to me when I was a teenager in England."

These two reports were happy exceptions, for I infrequently see the long-range impact of my sermons. We can't see into the heart, where beliefs, values, priorities, and devotions change, so a pastor's preaching may bring about significant spiritual breakthroughs that can't be quantified in the year-end report.

● *Felt needs and real needs.* I know I can get a quick response if I preach to felt needs, but that doesn't mean I've preached successfully.

Needy people focus on symptoms, not diseases. A sermon on self-esteem may temporarily boost people's self-confidence, but if we fail to give an antibiotic for the underlying problems — pride or lack of faith — it's malpractice. Symptom-oriented sermons, like candy medicine, make people smile, but people go away as sick as ever.

I do address felt needs, but primarily as an entrée to people's real needs, for that's the seed bed of the most successful preaching.

● *Spiritual variables.* God's Word always achieves its intended purpose, but wielding it is not an exact science. In some ways we resemble farmers who intentionally burn parts of their fields; fire breaks out in unanticipated ways. Sometimes after a sermon bombed, someone will say I helped them tremendously. And sometimes we help people in spite of what we said or what they heard.

I once preached a sermon from the King James Version about the Lord being our "shield and buckler." A woman wrote me saying she was greatly helped by my teaching on the Lord being her shield and *butler*. She was encouraged knowing that the Lord was standing at her shoulder ready to help!

We must never assume, then, that the sermon is ours to make or break. In the 1800s a famous organist traveled from town to town giving concerts. In each town he hired a boy to pump the organ during the concert. After one performance, he couldn't shake the boy, who followed him back to his hotel.

"Well, we had a great concert tonight, didn't we?" said the boy.

"*I* had a great concert," replied the maestro. "Go home!"

The next night, halfway through a fugue, the organ quit. The little boy stuck his head around the corner of the organ, grinned, and said, "We aren't havin' a very good concert tonight, are we?"

If God isn't pumping when we're preaching, nothing happens.

Seven Signs

How a sermon is received, then, is but one criterion of a successful sermon, and not a reliable one at that. Instead, I put more emphasis on how a sermon is prepared and preached. I look for seven signs in examining my sermons. If I've fulfilled most or all of these criteria in a sermon, I've gone a long way toward preaching a successful sermon.

Let me summarize them briefly, illustrating them with a sermon that did, in fact, receive a favorable congregational response: *What About Shaky Marriages?*

● *God centered.* My primary concern in preaching is to glorify God through his Son. That's my concern even in practical sermons, like *What About Shaky Marriages?*

I bridged the practical and theological as I discussed the difference between the Greek words for *love:* "You can have all kinds of *philia* and *eros* and still not approach the love that makes marriage work best. The third word for love in Greek is *agape.* This word describes God's love for us." Later I said, "The Bible teaches that *agape* love is directly related to the work of the Holy Spirit."

At the close of the message, I said, "The Spirit of God begins to shed his love in our hearts. There's a fundamental spiritual dimension here that must never be shortchanged: the dedication to go on loving and being devoted to the One who is the source of all love."

The sermon focused on a human problem — shaky marriages — but I still wanted to point to God as the source of marriage-healing love.

• *Biblically based.* A successful sermon comes from God's Word, not my or someone else's experience, not another book or article. A biblical text cannot be a pretext: I can't read the text then ignore it for the rest of the message (the preaching equivalent of bait-and-switch).

With literature on marriage abounding, I could have easily based my marriage sermon on psychological principles. That would have helped people, I'm sure. But I wanted to go even deeper, so I based it on the characteristics of love described in 1 Corinthians 13. I took each quality of love — love is kind, love is patient, love rejoices in the right, and so on — and simply explained and applied it.

This doesn't mean that all my sermons are verse-by-verse expositions. Still, I try to ground every point in a clear inference from the text.

• *People directed.* I delivered a series of expository sermons on 1 Peter some time ago. After a year of that, one staff member commented, "You're getting bogged down. People are losing interest."

I had sensed the congregation's interest flagging, but I had idealistically been thinking, *This is God's Word. It's eternal truth. As long as I explain it and help people apply it, fruit will result.*

When my colleague brought it to my attention, I realized I couldn't ignore the problem. If people are tired, bored, or distracted, my sermon will be hampered even if other factors are in my favor.

Over the years I've become increasingly aware that people were not made for the sermon but the sermon for people. Successful sermons help people both with eternal life and daily life, both with felt needs and real needs. They don't deal just with ideas, principles, and Scriptures, but with people, emotions, problems, families, money, work.

Furthermore, I've found that from the beginning I must communicate clearly that the sermon is for them. If I give twenty minutes of exposition and then try to tack on an application, I will have lost most of my listeners. So right in the introduction, I usually tell people how the sermon will relate to their concerns.

In *What About Shaky Marriages?* I began like this:

"Clint Eastwood made a movie called *Heartbreak Ridge*. I'm not a Clint Eastwood fan, but there is a side story in that movie where Eastwood — the 24-year-veteran marine gunnery sergeant, Congressional Medal of Honor winner — has lost his wife: she's left him and doesn't want anything to do with him. This big macho man is quite pathetic. He doesn't know what to do, so he starts buying women's magazines. You have a remarkable picture of Clint Eastwood reading women's magazines to find out what on earth his wife really wants. The tragedy is that it's perfectly obvious to everybody else but not to Clint. Marriages are shaky. People involved in shaky marriages don't understand some very basic facts about marriage."

● *Intellectually competent.* A successful sermon appeals to the mind by being logical and credible. It coherently interprets Scripture, and it develops in a way that makes sense to listeners.

To be intellectually competent, a sermon often must nuance thought and make subtle distinctions.

In my marriage sermon, in speaking on the phrase, "Love is not jealous," I said, "Now this poses a problem. We know that God is love, and we know that God is jealous. How can Paul say that love is not jealous?

"There are different kinds of jealousy. There's a holy jealousy committed to protecting that which is dear. I protect Jill. If people get after her, they don't just deal with her; they deal with me. If they get on her case, that's my case. If they criticize her for what she's doing, or for what she doesn't do, then I will handle that for her. (I'm getting ticked just thinking about it!) That is holy jealousy.

"There is a jealousy that goes beyond protecting and becomes possessive. That possessiveness becomes a power that dominates the other person with little interest in the other's well-being. In some marriages you'll find one partner or the other so committed to what they expect of the other person, they won't even listen to the other person's desires. Their jealousy has become destructive possessiveness. Love is not jealous."

● *Emotionally moving.* Successful sermons address not only the mind but the heart.

In explaining the phrase, "Love is not rude," I said, "Rudeness despises people. Rudeness denigrates people. If it goes on long enough, rudeness destroys people.

"You remember Archie Bunker. What angered me so much was Bunker's attitude toward his wife. He constantly called her 'silly cow!' That woman, as portrayed in the program, was totally beaten. I don't think he physically abused her, but she lived with constant verbal rudeness and denigration, which for all intents and purposes destroyed her. She had come to the conclusion that she was a silly cow. Bunker was clearly limited in his love for his wife. Love couldn't possibly be rude."

Archie Bunker's treatment of his wife would offend most listeners; it would strike at an emotional level, as it did me, and that's one reason I used him as an illustration.

● *Volitionally challenging.* A successful sermon also appeals to the will. It doesn't just spew information or inspire emotions; it calls people to live in a new way.

"We are not to assume," I said, "that *agape* love is simply the result of the Holy Spirit working on passive people: I stand around, and the Holy Spirit loves you through me. It doesn't work like that. You will notice that the Bible also speaks of *agape* as a responsibility. This wonderful passage in 1 Corinthians 13 concludes with the words, 'Follow the way of love.'

"Unfortunately, whoever divided the Bible into chapters shoved that phrase into the next chapter, but after Paul talks about love, we are told to follow the way of love. The words translated 'follow the way of' mean 'to hunt or to pursue relentlessly' — to target a goal and fulfill it. *Agape* love is the result of the Holy Spirit operating within our lives, but it is also the result of making a commitment to target somebody with *agape* love and loving them relentlessly."

• *Practically comprehensible.* A successful sermon is as clear and useful as the morning paper. My favorite Scripture about preaching is Nehemiah 8:8, "They read from the Book of the Law of God, making it clear and giving the meaning so that the people could understand what was being read." I'm best at "making it clear and giving the meaning" when I show how a biblical principle looks in daily life. Here's how I did that in one passage of my marriage sermon:

"When things go wrong in an intimate relationship, as they inevitably do, we carefully recall and rehearse what went wrong. If we continue to rehearse in our own minds what went wrong, we will find ourselves resenting what went wrong. Resentment builds until we are concerned about revenge. Sometimes we have to recognize that resenting and revenge seeking have absolutely nothing to do with what the Spirit of God wants to work in our lives: a willingness to forgive as Christ has forgiven us. Love does not keep records."

Growing Continuously

These seven criteria are not the end of it. Successful preaching cannot be reduced to a formula. It's a dynamic process, and an essential part of the process is the preacher's growth.

It's easy to stop growing, of course. You've been churning out one or more sermons a week for years. It takes increasingly more work to make slight improvement. People respond well to your messages. The time may come when you say to yourself, *I've got this thing nailed down* or *This is as good as I'm going to get.*

Some preachers resemble many NFL first-round draft choices, those naturally talented athletes who never reach their full potential. Success has always come easily, so they never had to exercise great discipline; they coast on their gifts.

Granted, in some facets of preaching, our growth will be limited or nil. I have never been comfortable preaching in large evangelistic settings where an "altar call" is expected, and I don't give invitations at Elmbrook Church. That's partly my personality; I am basically a shy, undemonstrative person who has never answered an altar call himself. I've been in situations where my hosts wanted me to give an invitation, and I tried, but I felt awkward.

But I work at growing in other areas. Warren Wiersbe observed in one interview that over the years my preaching has changed. It no longer is straight exposition, he said, but has become earthed where people live. Over the years I have worked hard at illustrating better.

I find continued growth comes best if I remember three things.

First, I want to build on my natural gifts. When Tom Landry, former coach of the Dallas Cowboys, saw running back Tony Dorsett play football for the first time, he turned to an assistant and said, "You don't coach that. You draft it." His point, of course, wasn't to quit coaching a talented runner, but that the best results come from working with talent.

Some preachers are gifted at evangelistic preaching, others at teaching. Others are relational in the pulpit, counseling people *en masse*. Others are natural exhorters, who can effectively challenge listeners to greater obedience. Some prefer expository preaching, others topical. Whatever your strength, major in it.

Enhancing strengths, however, still leaves room for experimentation with new things, for stretching ourselves. We don't know what we can do until we've tried.

In the sixties the last thing I wanted was to work with youth. "That's not my strength," I told people. "I can't do it." Eventually a friend more or less shamed me into helping him with a coffee house ministry to the teenagers of Britain.

My friend, a physician, had surveyed hundreds of school kids and found that they were interested in Jesus but totally disinterested in church. He said to me, "You have a gift for reaching kids with the gospel, but you aren't even close to most of them because you preach in church settings. So if we are going to fish for people, you and I need to go where the fish are. They're in the coffee houses."

He was right. I knew it, so we went. Eventually I developed my own ministry called Coffeebar Evangelism, and people wrote me from around the world, asking how they could do it. Speaking to youth became the focus of my ministry.

I also try to learn from other preachers. Copying others is a mistake, but comparing and contrasting can benefit us in several ways.

First, other preachers show us possibilities.

In my upbringing, most of the things that went on outside the church were considered "worldly." I was interested in these off-limits subjects — sports, drama, and literature — but they played no role in my preaching. Then I heard Paul Rees, an evangelical leader of the last generation. He was not only interested and knowledgeable about such things, he talked about them in sermons. In him I heard a preacher who was not only interested in the culture but who found illustrations of biblical truth there.

In addition, other preachers model preaching values. In my formative years as a preacher, I admired Alan Redpath and Stephen Olford for their fire. Their messages gripped them and me. John Stott's preaching has always challenged me to be clear, to lay out the Word in orderly fashion. The sermons of G. Campbell Morgan, Charles Spurgeon, and John Wesley strike me with their high regard for Scripture and their passion to get the Word out to people.

Third, I weigh feedback heavily. While I don't evaluate my own preaching in a structured way, I do pay close attention to what others tell me.

My wife, Jill, reminds me of my need to keep working at application, the weakest area of my preaching. That's because I wrongly assume others are like me. I learn through principles; give me the principle, and I'll figure out how to apply it. Jill reminds me that most listeners need specifics: "First you do this, second you do this, third you do that."

Though the comments of others can sometimes be unnerving, I find safety in this process. When preachers veer onto a tangent or fall into a rut, it's usually because they have secluded themselves from a trusted circle's healthy feedback.

When I was a teenager, a man asked me, "How old are you?"

"Seventeen," I replied.

"It's time you were preaching."

"I can't preach."

"Have you tried?"

"No."

"Well then, you can't possibly know you can't do it."

That's how I got started in the pulpit. And since then, I've worked hard to preach effectively. But I've also learned to trust, as well.

Farmers plow their lands, plant their seed, and then go home to bed, awaiting God's germinating laws to work. Surgeons only cut; God heals. I must give my full energy to doing my part in the pulpit, but the ultimate success of my preaching rests in God.

The most striking thing about highly effective leaders is how little they have in common. What one swears by, another warns against. But one trait stands out: the willingness to risk.

— *Larry Osborne*

CHAPTER FIVE

Taking Risks

Rich had just taken the pastorate of one of the largest churches in his denomination. He had experienced tremendous success in his previous church, a church plant that had grown to over 2,000 under his innovative, risk-taking style of leadership. Rich entered his new ministry assuming a long and bright future.

To his dismay, he found that a few arbitrary decisions, small mistakes in judgment, and the launching of a couple of pet projects took on epic proportions. Things that had been ignored in Memphis suddenly became a cause for impeachment in Minnesota.

Baffled, he tried to wrestle more and more control from his opponents. But instead of gaining more authority and freedom, he gained only more enemies. Within eighteen months he resigned, a crushed and confused pastor, wondering how someone who had been hailed as an innovative, risk-taking leader in one setting could be written off as an incompetent, wild-eyed gambler in another.

What is it that causes a leader to succeed in one setting and fail in another? More to the point, what makes a leader great?

For years I've studied leaders and their ministries hoping to get answers. I've focused on the highly successful, looking for their secrets, which I could apply to my own life and ministry. But what I've found has surprised me. Instead of secrets, principles, and patterns that guarantee success, I've found amazing diversity. While there are certainly some common threads to be found, the most striking thing about highly effective leaders is how little they have in common. What one swears by, another warns against.

Still, one trait stands out: the willingness to risk. Highly successful leaders ignore conventional wisdom and take chances. Their stories inevitably include a defining moment or key decision when they took a significant risk and thereby experienced a breakthrough.

But herein lies the rub. My study of leaders and ministries has also focused on another group — those who have failed miserably — and among them I've also found a common trait: the willingness to risk. They too ignore conventional wisdom, go against the odds. But in their cases, the results were tragic, not triumphant.

So what gives? What separates a successful risk taker from a bankrupt gambler?

I've come to believe it's the ability to distinguish between a prudent risk and a wild-eyed gamble. To increase my ability to discern the difference, I've learned to ask myself five key questions before taking ministry out on a limb.

Who Else Has Done It?

My first question is always "Who else has been there?"

Solomon said, "There's nothing new under the sun," and I

believe him. So before I set out on a risky venture, I've learned to search out those who've already gone down that path or a similar one.

By asking what went well and what went wrong, I can usually pinpoint where the dangers lie, which takes much of the risk out of a risky situation.

A couple of years ago, without warning, our church, which had been renting facilities from another church, lost its lease. We were forced into an emergency building program, with no lead time and no money. Knowing that time and money are two vital ingredients to a successful program and that any building program is risky in its own right, I was, to say the least, concerned.

Due to our short time frame, purchasing land and building a traditional facility from scratch was not an option. So we hunted for an empty shopping center, industrial building, or warehouse capable of being converted into a church. In addition, we wanted one large enough to allow for future growth.

Finally we found a facility that might work. It was large enough, had adequate parking, and fell within an area zoned for church use. It was also the only facility within fifteen miles to meet those criteria.

Still, we had no margin for error. It would so stretch our finances that even the slightest time delay or cost overrun would break us. I wondered if I shouldn't go for a smaller place, of which there were a number.

Before making any recommendations to the congregation, I decided to talk to other pastors who had already turned a retail or industrial site into a church. To my surprise, I heard the same thing over and over. Their delay and cost overruns could be traced to one of three areas:

1. Architectural plans. To save money, many had used an in-house architect or draftsman to draw up their plans. Inexperience in designing large-occupancy buildings led to long delays as they redrew the plans numerous times to comply with the stricter building codes governing large-occupancy buildings.

2. City approval. I also had heard stories aplenty about the

horrors of trying to gain a zoning change or municipal approval to build. One church leader told of waiting two years before receiving a final go-ahead. But in each case where the process had snarled, I found the church had depended upon an inexperienced lay leader or staff member to navigate the bureaucratic maze. The result was a series of wrong turns and dead ends before finally arriving at their destination.

3. Volunteer labor. Everywhere I heard the same story. Many volunteered to help; few actually showed up. Churches depending heavily on volunteer labor spoke of saving money but losing time. In one case, the construction took a year longer than anticipated.

I was amazed how similar the stories were. Once I heard their stories, however, I took heart. I now knew where the predictable risks lay, which meant we could devise a plan to minimize them.

I recommended to the board and church that we go for it. We spent a little more money on our architect, hired a professional consultant to guide us through the bureaucratic maze, and counted on little if any help from volunteers.

The result was a new facility — finished on time and under budget — capable of handling not only the people we already had but a lot of new folks as well.

How Bad Can It Get?

Another question I've learned to ask before taking a significant risk is "What's the worst thing that can happen here?" and "Can I live with it?"

If I can't live with it, it's seldom a risk worth taking.

Both my theology and life taught me long ago that whatever can go wrong, will go wrong. It has something to do with what the Bible calls the Fall and the world calls Murphy's Law. By either name it's ignored at great peril.

That was Nick's mistake. Four years after planting a new church, he felt he was at a dead end. No matter what he tried, the church couldn't break the two-hundred barrier. Every growth spurt was followed by an exodus of folks who were upset over some minor issue or were moving out of the area.

To Nick, the major culprit was an inadequate facility. Lacking the people and money to purchase their own site, they had to rent a run-down community hall. From the lingering smell of stale beer to the peeling paint and dim lighting, the facility repelled rather than attracted new people.

When the pastor of a small struggling church in the area suggested the two churches merge, Nick was intrigued. Though they represented different denominations, the differences were minor, centered on polity, not doctrine. In addition, the other church had a facility and one hundred members. To Nick, it looked like a risk worth taking. If all went well, it would solve his two greatest problems: the lack of a permanent facility and the two-hundred barrier.

So he pushed ahead, lobbying his board and congregation until they finally agreed to the merger.

But Nick made a critical mistake. He was so focused on the potential benefits, he failed to seriously consider what might go wrong. To him, trusting God meant focusing only on the upside. Worst case scenarios were an exercise for those who lacked faith.

But there are drawbacks. Nick failed to realize successful mergers are rare. More often it means one church will get swallowed by the other, and Nick hadn't asked himself if he could accept being swallowed.

A year later that's exactly what happened. Nick found himself functioning more and more as an assistant to the other pastor. His influence with the board and congregation waned. Finally, feeling bitter and betrayed, he resigned.

The worst thing that could happen had happened, and he couldn't live with it. He now looks back on the good old days when he pastored a church of less than two hundred in a run-down, rented, community hall.

There's another advantage to asking, "What can go wrong, and can I live with it?" Sometimes it helps me realize a risk is worth taking but not just yet.

That's what happened when we changed our worship style.

When I first came to the church, we were a preaching station. Our services consisted of song, commercial, song, commercial, and then a forty-five minute sermon. From the beginning I felt if we were going to reach our community, we needed to make worship a higher priority; we also needed to depend less upon traditional hymns and more on contemporary musical styles.

There was only one problem. Our 120 people liked it as it was. That's why they came. Only a few wanted to change.

At that point, it would have been foolish to risk a sudden, major shift in worship style. While the upside of such a change was the possibility of reaching more people, the downside was too much to bear: a potential mass exodus at a time when we barely had enough people to pay the bills and keep the place open.

So I waited, making only incremental changes. Four years later we finally reached critical mass. We had enough people in the pews; losing a few wouldn't kill us. And the ones most likely to go were long-time Christians who could quickly find another church with music more to their liking. More importantly, those likely to go were doing little to help us reach the community. Few of them had brought anyone to church other than an out-of-town relative or a friend who was already a Christian.

So we made the change. We did lose some people. But it was a loss we could live with it. And in our case, we not only lived with it, we flourished.

Can I Try It on for Size?

A third question I ask myself before taking a risk is "Can I give it a trial run?"

Obviously that's not always feasible, as when hiring staff or building a facility. But I've found many risky decisions (or at least parts of decisions) can be tried on for size before I commit to them.

A trial run can save heartache. It can turn a stupid decision into nothing more than a popped trial balloon, blunting the impact of what would otherwise be a major failure.

Len was a high energy, do-it-right-now type. That trait served him well as the new pastor of a small suburban church. Under his leadership it grew from 75 to nearly 600 in four years. But then the growth stopped.

Len had a hard time adjusting. He felt more and more like a failure. Convinced God had more growth in store for the church, he read books and attended conferences about spurring a church on to greater heights. When Len came home from one of those conferences, he was full of enthusiasm and vision for the future. "The key" was a new approach to ministry that had produced phenomenal results at the church hosting the conference.

Len put on a full-court press with his board. The board agreed to follow his lead, and within weeks Len embraced a new preaching style, an aggressive evangelistic outreach program, and a more authoritarian approach to leadership. Len knew the changes would meet some resistance, but he felt sure an influx of new believers would more than make up for the loss of a few opponents.

He was wrong. One year later, attendance logged in at 300. What had gone wrong?

An unforeseen cultural clash. Len was emulating a ministry located in a predominantly blue-collar community where a forty-hour workweek was the norm, leaving many members with significant free time for a high-commitment, volunteer ministry. In addition, they were open and responsive to an authoritarian style of leadership.

Len's church was located in an upper-class neighborhood. His parishioners were highly educated, well-compensated professionals who worked fifty to seventy hours a week. They rebelled at even a hint of strong-armed leadership.

By the time Len realized what was going on, it was too late. Even after he shelved new programs and emphases, he couldn't bring back those who had left.

Len's story contrasts sharply with another church and pastor I know. There too, the church had plateaued, leading to a search for new ways to get things moving again.

That pastor also flew home from a week-long conference, ecstatic about a new ministry model. He, too, gathered his board and began to sell them on his new vision. But instead of putting forward his suggested changes as permanent, he suggested a trial period. So, for six months, one Sunday a month, the church experimented with "seeker" services.

It soon became obvious the changes wouldn't turn the church around. While no one left over the changes, only the pastor and a few key leaders were excited about the new direction.

They decided to scrap the idea. Although the leaders were discouraged over their failed experiment, it didn't sink the church.

How Much Rope Do I Have?

A fourth question I ask is "How much room do I have for error?"

When I came to North Coast, I failed to ask this question and nearly hung myself.

I followed a much-loved founding pastor. The tight-knit congregation had not yet finished the grieving process when I arrived and began making changes. Because the changes were small, I figured the risks were minimal.

They weren't. Inconsequential changes in the worship service, bulletin, and church calendar created an uproar. One family said they were leaving because the service no longer ended with a closing hymn. Another because I failed to schedule the annual New Year's Eve party. Still another asked where I intended to send my kids to school and then left when I gave the wrong answer — this despite the fact that my wife and I hadn't yet had any children!

I was left reeling. My stomach churned every time I heard a phone ring, conditioned, like Pavlov's dog, to expect the worst.

Since then, I've learned that the amount of risk in a decision is directly related to the quality of my relationship with the people affected. When the relationships are deep, my margin for error is great. When the relationships are shallow or strained, there may not even be a margin for error.

Frankly, I no longer worry about the effects of my changing the bulletin, an annual program, or how I take the offering. I seldom worry about the fallout from a new ministry or a potential change in direction. After thirteen years, a measure of success, and a couple of major crises successfully navigated, I've acquired enough rope to outlive a few failures or misguided decisions. I'm not cavalier, but I'm aware that as my margin for error has increased, so has my freedom to take risks. Failure doesn't look so bad when I know it won't be fatal.

In some situations, naturally, a newly arrived leader has all the rope he needs from day one. When the church is in a crisis or is looking to the new leader to be a white knight riding to the rescue, the risk of making major changes is often less than the risk of standing pat. Usually, though, it's wise to consider first how much rope you have.

How Clearly Has God Spoken?

The last question I ask before climbing out on a limb is "How clearly has God spoken?"

The clearer God's direction, the greater the risk I'm willing to take. Like Abraham, mounting his donkey to go sacrifice his son Isaac, or Peter, stepping out on the water to go to Jesus, I want to obey when the Lord speaks clearly, no matter the risk.

The hard part is deciphering whether God has spoken clearly or I've merely baptized my ideas and desires. Sometimes it's hard to tell. That's why I use all the questions we've been looking at. I believe they go a long way in determining God's will for our church. But on top of those questions, I want to be open to a clear word from the Lord.

Sometimes God's leading is so clear it needs to be followed, regardless of how it matches up with anybody's criteria. One of the best decisions I've ever made (and one of the greatest risks I've ever taken) flew in the face of all my risk questions.

At the time, we were looking to hire our first full-time associate. I wanted the person to preach about 20 percent of our Sunday morning services.

The person I presented to our elder board was a member of our church, in fact, one of the elders. He was also a close friend. He was a godly man, had a Bible degree from a respected Christian college, and had taught a number of home Bible studies over the years.

So far so good. But he'd also just been fired from his post as a Bible teacher and administrator at a local Christian school. He had no seminary education, and he'd never preached a sermon in his life. To top it off, the one time I'd heard him teach a Bible study, it was boring.

On the surface, he was not the most qualified person for the position, and he would enter it with some considerable liabilities. A number of the elders resisted the idea of hiring him. But one night, as I was driving home from a meeting that concerned this decision, I felt God clearly tell me we were to hire him. The message didn't come in an audible voice, but it might as well have: I felt a powerful and deep sense of conviction that this was the man for our church. I couldn't explain it, nor could I explain it away.

When I shared my experience with the elders, they graciously trusted me and acted in faith, and he was hired.

Today, all in our church agree that Mike has been one of God's greatest gifts to our ministry. Along with providing outstanding leadership to a thriving home fellowship ministry, he's become an excellent preacher. He now preaches over 30 percent of the time, and on most of those occasions, I'm in the audience, not on the road.

Risk taking is not an option if we want to be effective in ministry. But it's vital that those risks be prudent. By asking these five questions, I've found it's possible to take risks without risking too much in the process.

PART 2
Relationships

Some decisions we'll never feel peace about until after they're made. The tranquility often comes after we've made the difficult choice.

— *Knute Larson*

CHAPTER SIX
Making the Right Moves

The candidating process for becoming pastor of The Chapel took fourteen months.

During the drawn-out ordeal, I slipped into a low-grade depression I couldn't shake, losing nineteen pounds. I felt guilty for even considering the idea of leaving my church in Ashland. After fifteen good years, I wondered if I were "deserting" that church. It felt like divorce.

Feeling discouraged and confused one day, I threw down what I knew to be a silly and desperate challenge before God: "Lord,

I'm going to turn on the car radio. Whatever this radio preacher says will be what you are saying to me."

I clicked on the dial, and the first words I heard were, "Go, I am sending you, and I will give you courage and what to say."

At first I laughed. Then I cried. Naturally, I wasn't going to let this "coincidence" or the voice of John MacArthur determine my future, but it did make me fidget.

A month later, still in depression, I put out another such unorthodox fleece. Late one evening, my wife and I were discussing the pros and cons of moving when I said, "Jeanine, I'm going to turn on *Haven of Rest*. Whatever is on the program tonight will give us the answer."

She smiled. (I would have said, "Baloney," if *she* had proposed it.)

I turned on the radio program only to hear the program's associate director explain why he was resigning and moving on to a new ministry.

"I have struggled with the issue of my indispensability," I recall him saying. "But I've come to the conclusion that God can replace me in this ministry. The work here will go on, so I must take this next step in my life."

We sat a few moments in silence, prayed, and tried to figure out if God or the enemy or coincidence was behind this.

I finally did accept the position at The Chapel, though not on the basis of those two happenstance radio messages (though they did play a role, I have to admit). Other factors, like the match between the church's needs and my gifts, the enthusiastic support of my family, and finally, my own desire to go, were the key factors.

The thought of moving can play havoc with our emotions, surging from paralysis to impatience. We know the decision to move has far-reaching consequences, perhaps for good, perhaps for ill. In fact, it's one of the toughest decisions pastors make. Here are some principles that have helped me think more clearly about such times.

When Leaving Is Wrong

A variety of things can stir up discontentment in our present ministries, but none by themselves is usually reason enough to leave a church. Here are some common frustrations that shouldn't necessarily point us down the road.

First, we shouldn't leave just because things aren't going well. Ray and Anne Ortlund give some excellent advice along these lines. Speaking to a gathering of pastors at The Chapel, they warned of the dangers of the ABZ Syndrome.

A pastor arrives at a church and enjoys a honeymoon period — stage-A. But inevitably the day comes when the honeymoon relationship sours. When the criticism starts, disillusionment can set in — stage-B. Pastors are then faced with the dilemma: "Do I stay and pray and gut it out?" or "Do I begin sending out my resume?"

The Ortlunds believe that if we stay and endure the pain of stage-B, we can eventually move into stage-C, where energy and enthusiasm for the ministry returns. As a result, we may even reenter stage-A once more, finding great contentment in our setting. It's possible to go through stages A, B, and C several times in one church.

However, those who find stage-B too uncomfortable often move directly into mode-Z. They decide staying is useless, pack their belongings, and do it over again in another setting. Unfortunately for many pastors, life is a series of A-B-Z experiences. They miss the joy of seeing God strengthen them through their trials and thus achieving genuine peace.

Second, we shouldn't leave just because we have to deal with an obstinate person or problem in the church. I remember a young pastor, a former intern with our church, telling me that he had decided to leave his church after only a year. The board chairman was unbearably aggravating.

"He won't allow me to lead the board in devotions before our meetings," the young pastor complained. "He's put me on notice that he's the board leader and that I'm the spiritual leader. Deciding who will give devotions, he says, is his responsibility."

"How often do you meet one-on-one with the chairman?" I asked.

"Well, ah, we don't meet," he replied.

I encouraged the young pastor to get together with his chairman once a month, even twice a month if possible, to nurture a more personal relationship.

The pastor followed through on my advice. Soon, he was giving devotions at the board meetings. Through their times together, the pastor communicated to the chairman he wasn't interested in power but genuine spiritual leadership.

Third, we can be tempted to move on because we're restless; we don't feel challenged. After eight years at my previous church, I felt some of this, as I mentioned in a previous chapter. While the church was growing stronger, I was growing restless.

Instead of looking for another ministry, though, I was able to assume responsibilities with our denominational headquarters. That additional challenge was all I needed to find contentment for seven more years.

For many pastors, simply adding another challenge such as writing or volunteering in the community can meet a need for personal growth and development. Restlessness seems to be a normal characteristic of ambitious people, but finding another arena to stretch our muscles often can be done without resigning our present situation.

When It's Time to Go

So what is a legitimate reason for leaving? Here are three good reasons for considering a change of scenery.

● *Holy ambition.* During the time I was deciding whether or not to come to Akron, a member at Ashland challenged me, asking, "Are you sure this isn't just your move up the corporate ladder?"

"Maybe it is," I replied. I was half-ashamed to say so, even though I think moving up the ladder can be a good thing. Ambition becomes destructive when we try to usurp control from God. Or when it drives us to walk over people or use churches. Or when ministry decisions degenerate into self-serving schemes and carefully manipulated calculations. In such cases ambition becomes another word for pride and rebellion.

I'm impressed with the parable of the talents, in which Christ rewarded those who took their talents and wisely invested them. To me, using our gifts to minister to more people or in a more receptive setting can be simply good stewardship, though numbers can never be the main consideration.

● *A special calling.* Some pastors have the unique skills of a church pioneer, who can build a church from the ground up. Others have proven to be specialists at interim pastorates, serving angry or hurting churches. (Some denominations insist that a church call an interim pastor following a long-term leader or in the midst of congregational turmoil.)

Others may simply not be as well-equipped to take a church to the next stage, though they may have been successful up to a certain point, so they move on.

● *Loss of vision.* When I'm asked the question, "When is it time to leave my church?" I usually reply, "When you lose your energy and vision for the church and can't get it back again."

Losing our vision can be traced to a sense of failure or fatigue brought on by conflict. Or it can be the result of completing the work you set out to do: the church has been successfully planted, the building program completed, or the transition from one era to another finished. If your original vision has been fulfilled, and another doesn't take its place, the time to leave may be near.

I would add this caveat: there's a difference between losing vision and failing to confront frustrating issues with wisdom or patience. Some matters take time to be resolved. Pastors generally leave too soon rather than stay too long.

The Heat Is On

As we consider moves, some fear is to be expected and desired; it helps us weigh such important decisions. But letting fear have its way can paralyze us.

While wrestling with the move to Akron, I was preparing to

run in a five-mile race. I had trained for months with a friend. We developed a good-natured rivalry and routinely sent each other anonymous notes, trying to "psych out" the other person before the big day. He signed his notes "Mercury"; I used "The Streak."

Just before race day, my friend presented me with a tee-shirt that said, "The Streak." On the back of the shirt was a large yellow stripe running down the spine.

Little did he know how close he had come to the truth about my feelings. The decision facing me whether to stay at Ashland or move to The Chapel had partially paralyzed me. I was terrified I might make the wrong choice, hurting the people I loved the most in the world. I thought I might be committing spiritual adultery! They had been loyal and loving. How could I consider abandoning them?

I gradually realized, though, that leaving a congregation is no more abandonment than a man or woman leaving family to get married. There is a time to stay and a time to move on. I had to learn to reframe my central question: not "Am I deserting these people?" but "What is the best way I can glorify God and help people, making the best use of my abilities?"

That, of course, elicited another fear — that I would not live in the center of God's will. I got over that fear once I realized that I didn't agree with the "dot theory" of God's will: God has a specific town, place, and address he desires to send us to; our challenge is to locate that dot on the map; until we locate it, we shouldn't go anywhere.

I suggest that for many decisions, some of them very important, God has not given us special instructions. Instead, he's given us latitude to make a decision, within the moral and spiritual boundaries set by Scripture. I'm to use my God-given wisdom to decide between alternatives, weighing such things as family concerns, the church's vision, and my own gifts. With many decisions, as long as I'm seeking to live faithfully, there may be two or three "godly" outcomes, ones God would approve of.

The nicest thing anyone said to me during that decision-making year was "You can't make a mistake." My good friend

George had said that, wanting me to realize that because I really wanted God's input and wanted to be used by God in this decision, I would be successful in God's eyes, no matter which path I took.

I now repeat that assurance frequently when I talk to others considering a similar change.

We not only have to contend with our fears but also our egos. While waiting for my present church to conclude their search, a church on the West Coast, convinced I was the right man to pastor their congregation (though I had never candidated there) voted unanimously to pursue me, telling me that coming there was God's will.

During the fourteen months I was talking with Akron, this California church continued to court me, calling, writing, and even visiting me.

"I can't go any further with you," I told them repeatedly, "until the Akron situation is resolved." But when things began to drag a bit in Ohio (I had not heard anything for months), I finally agreed to travel to their church and speak — with the understanding I was not a candidate.

That was a mistake.

As soon as I arrived, I fell in love with the church. That week we went through several quasi-interviews, always qualifying our meetings with the statement, "But of course, this isn't an official interview."

Looking back I regret ever having become involved with another church while the process in Akron was still up in the air. Obviously, I eventually decided against it, but in the meantime, it only confused matters for everyone. Frankly, it's nice to be courted, and it's hard to say no.

Now when I get a phone call or letter to consider a church, knowing I should be here, I say, "No, thank you," rather quickly so there is no hint of starting what cannot be finished.

A third temptation is to fail to do one's homework.

After seminary and two years as an associate, I had agreed to candidate at a church I knew little about. After only a brief meeting with their committee, I consented to a candidating weekend. I arrived on a Friday evening, and within ten minutes, I knew I had made a mistake.

The people were great, but I sensed we spoke different languages, especially when they talked about church evangelism and a few areas of practical theology.

I hung around through Sunday morning, but as it approached, I grew increasingly uncomfortable. During the service, a "down-home" gospel group sang the special music, which symbolized to me our deep differences. I prefer classical, traditional, or contemporary music. Well, this number never seemed to end.

Afterwards a church trustee invited me to his home for lunch. During the meal, he said, "The people like you." I nodded weakly.

After the meal, he stood up and said, "I've got a surprise for you." He put on an album by the group that had performed the special music.

"How do you like their music?" he asked with a big grin.

I groped for words. My wife, obviously interested in my predicament, emerged from their kitchen just to see how I would handle the question. I finally mumbled something bland like, "They obviously enjoy their ministry." I could have saved myself a lot of awkwardness had I investigated the church more thoroughly before agreeing to candidate.

The Downside of Moving Up

Life is a series of trade-offs. Though most of us think of moving up to churches with larger staffs and more ministry opportunities, moving to a larger congregation may not be for everyone. Several considerations should be kept in mind when contemplating such a move.

● *The pastor-Peter principle.* Lyle Schaller has identified the different roles a pastor must play as a church gets larger. Pastors, for example, may find themselves moving from being a "gardener" (keeping the place weeded) to becoming a "rancher" (supervising the work on two thousand acres).

The disconcerting news, to some anyway, is that good

gardeners don't necessarily do well at managing a ranch. Thus if we're not honest about our strengths and weaknesses, we may find ourselves in a place that doesn't match our abilities. That will only hurt us and the church.

• *Three roles in one.* When I took on my present church, I discovered I had to become three persons in one. (No comparison to the Trinity intended at all!)

First, I became the president of a large corporation. A great deal of my time is now spent on staff, vision, and business issues. I read financial summaries and check the compass much more than in a small church.

I also became a shepherd of a large flock. I help direct the spiritual lives of a congregation where I don't know everyone by name. When I pastored a smaller church, I knew everyone I visited in the hospital. Now, many people are anonymous to me. Sometimes that feels uncomfortable to them and me, because a part of me wants to shepherd people one by one.

Furthermore, the larger the church, the more specialized the people problems tend to be. When I do have pastoral opportunities, I find that I spend much of my time with either "leaders" or "needers." The former are staff people and lay leaders. The latter are people who, because of their highly visceral needs, refuse to talk to anyone else.

Finally, I became a guest speaker to a large fringe group. This is my "Bible conference" and evangelism ministry, which, when a church gets over four or five hundred, becomes part of the pastor's job description. These are people who attend church only occasionally or hear me only when I speak at a civic function.

Most of the time, I enjoy all three roles. Each is a challenge and stretches me, but the combination is not for everyone.

• *Loss of intimacy.* As I mentioned in an earlier chapter, it's hard to stay connected with as many people as I once did. It was much easier to be a "people person" when I pastored a smaller church. In a larger church, I'm forced to surrender much of the shepherding tasks to others in the church. As a result I wind up losing a certain amount of intimacy. I do work closely with many people, but I can't help everyone who asks for help with their special ministry or program.

The Myth of Perfect Peace

Strange as it sounds, seeking complete peace of mind before saying yes to another position is an unwise and unreasonable expectation. We'll never feel peace about some decisions until they are made. The tranquility often comes after we've made the difficult choice. That was the case when I accepted the call to The Chapel.

The long journey to that peace began one day while I was vacationing in Michigan. While a colleague and I were walking along a beach, I stopped at a phone to pick up my messages. The church secretary informed me I had received a post card from a church in Akron.

"Do you want me to throw it away?" she asked.

"No," I said. "Keep it until I get back home."

When I returned home, I responded to the postcard and discovered their candidating process involved nine steps. Each step required a unanimous vote from the search committee of eighteen.

During that time, I began keeping a journal. In it I identified some doors that I believed had to open in order for me to accept the call.

One door was a deep desire on my part to go there. I wanted to feel a passion to serve that church if I was going to go through the pain of changing churches. This evolved slowly.

Another door involved persuading a local bank to turn our church's current construction mortgage into a permanent mortgage. The bank president had already informed me that if I left the church, they would not renew the mortgage. But when our board of elders met with the bank directors to discuss the issue, the bank eventually changed its mind. We received a letter from its president saying, "We believe the church is strong, and the leadership is not vested in one man alone." Another door had just swung open.

Still another door was the agreement of my family. As they visited the city and began thinking about the possibility of moving, my kids said, "Dad, you'd be crazy if you didn't take this opportunity." My wife was equally enthusiastic about the idea. She urged me to keep responding to their interest. They regretted a possible move, but they still encouraged me.

During the actual candidating week between two Sundays, I decided to add a final — the eleventh — door to my list.

"I'm not going there unless I get a 94 percent affirmative vote," I told my wife.

She looked at me for a moment and then replied with her first anger about my handling of the moving process: "Knute, I'm afraid you're playing games with God. If you don't want to go, why don't you just admit it?"

I didn't know why I had chosen 94 percent, but I said it, and I thought maybe I meant it! When the church eventually voted on the second Sunday, two church leaders involved in the candidating process stopped by our motel and told us the results: 95.7 percent in favor.

My wife and children cheered. "Well, that settles it," they said. "Here we go!"

But I was still skeptical. "I don't know yet," I replied somberly. "I still don't have peace about it."

I retreated to my bedroom and lay down. After nine different steps, fourteen months, and two weeks of preaching at the church, I still didn't know what to say. But I had told the church chairman I would give him my answer within two hours of his call to me.

For the next two hours, with hands folded like a cadaver, I lay on my bed, trying to decide what to do. I didn't want to make the call, but at five minutes to four, I got up, went to the phone, and dialed the chairman's number.

"We're coming."

My kids applauded, my wife hugged me, but my only emotion was the same old depression I had carried for so long. A part of me knew I had made the right decision. But it certainly didn't feel right. Immediately we drove back to our home church, and I delivered my resignation at the end of the evening service.

(The church knew where we were because I had chosen to announce the candidating one month before, knowing people hate surprises; in addition, I sought their prayers for wisdom.)

Five weeks later, our last day at the church, the congregation held a farewell reception. We stood in line for nearly two hours, hugging and crying with the people. My depression still had not lifted.

During the sixty-five minute drive from our old church to Akron, a remarkable thing happened. My depression lifted like a cloud. When we pulled into the driveway of our temporary new home, I had the wonderful feeling of being my old self again. I don't know if the healing was directly from God or if it was just that the ordeal of deciding was finally over. But I finally found the peace I had been seeking.

While I never received a direct call to go to Akron in the form of a theophany, God did work through the long, slow, and deliberate process (including a couple of radio messages!) to convince me to accept the call from The Chapel. In the end, common sense, good counsel, hours of prayer, and numerous green lights encouraged me to move.

I now rest in the fact that in the Bible I find a lot more promises from God indicating that he'll shepherd me than commands to find his specific will! Our main call is to keep our hearts pure and open to him, wherever we go.

In calling me to get married, God called me to divide my
time and energy between home and ministry.
— *Larry Osborne*

CHAPTER SEVEN
Between
Ministry
and Family

George Whitefield, the greatest evangelist of the eighteenth
century, once wrote happily, "I believe it is God's will that I should
marry." But he was concerned: "I pray God that I may not have a
wife till I can live as though I had none."

Whitefield, it seems, granted his own wish.

During his week-long honeymoon in his bride's home, he
preached twice a day in the surrounding countryside. Other than
two trips with him, his wife, Elizabeth, remained in their London
home during his constant travels (he crossed the Atlantic thirteen

times in his ministry). Once he was away from her for over two years.

When his 4-month-old son died, Whitefield did not stop ministry; he preached three more times before the funeral and was preaching as the bells rang for the funeral service itself.

From Whitefield's perspective, marriage and ministry were a troublesome mix. He sometimes spoke about marriage as if it were less of a blessing and more of a curse. He once wrote, "O for that blessed time when we shall neither marry nor be given in marriage, but be as the angels of God."

As for his wife's part, she seemed to have been equally unhappy, though she unfairly put the blame on herself: "I have been nothing but a load and burden to him."

A man who lived with the couple in their later years put it as tactfully as any: "He did not intentionally make his wife unhappy."

The call of God is a powerful force, which if not monitored, becomes all consuming, ripping us away from our earthly commitments. Neglecting spouse and children, of course, is never intentional. But it happens, too often and too easily.

The Fuller Institute of Church Growth recently conducted a survey among clergy, finding that close to 80 percent believed ministry adversely affected their families; 33 percent identified it as an outright hazard.

None of us wants to be a success at church and a failure at home. But it often seems as if the requirements of successful ministry and a successful home life are at odds. Both demand enormous attention and energy. Both are vitally important. Here are some strategies I use to try to give due attention to both.

Front-End Alignment

Every schoolteacher knows the importance of being tough with students the first week of school: the boundaries must be established on day one.

The front end of a pastorate is also the place to properly align church and family expectations.

When I candidated at North Coast Church, I set a precedent when I announced my wife would not be participating in the congregational question-and-answer period planned for my candidating weekend. I explained that she would be glad to stand when introduced, but I did not want her invited to join me on the stage. Nancy has never enjoyed public speaking (in fact, the very thought terrifies her); this seemed the right time to clarify that. My announcement drew some puzzled expressions from members of the pulpit committee, but they agreed to go along.

The temptation, though, is to do just the opposite. In the early effort to win the hearts of our people, we let the congregation heap on us expectations we know we can't live with in the long run — visiting every member, being at every meeting, accepting every invitation out. Later, when family pressure gets too great, we try to back away, upsetting people who don't understand our sudden reluctance.

Another way I've learned to protect my family on the front end is by making it difficult for people to meet with me in the evenings.

If someone calls the office and wants to schedule an appointment, the conversation often goes like this:

"Pastor, I need to talk with you. I need some help."

"Sure. What's the earliest date you could schedule an afternoon meeting?"

"I can't meet with you in the afternoon. I don't get off work until 5:00 or 6:00."

"Well, I try to avoid evening meetings, if at all possible. Otherwise my kids would never see me. What's the earliest time you could get off work?"

"I don't know, perhaps 3:00 or 3:30."

"Great, let's make it 3:30." Then I will often add, "I appreciate your flexibility."

Once in a while, though, someone will call who insists an afternoon meeting is impossible.

"Really?" I'll say. "They won't let you off any earlier?"

"Oh no. There's just no way my boss will let me."

That's the time I suddenly become available. "Okay, I'll see you at 6:00."

The result is that everybody is happy: the person needing my attention, my family, and me. It's always easier to give something away (like an evening) than it is to take it back.

Feedback You Need

I regularly check with my spouse and children to monitor how ministry is impacting them. I find my children are more likely to give a straight answer than is my wife. Spouses can feel unspiritual — as if they're taking us away from God's work — for complaining about our being gone so much.

So once a year I sit down with my wife and simply ask, "Do you feel like a pastor's wife?"

If she says, "No," then I say, "Good. We can do this for another year."

Here's what I mean by "pastor's wife": one who routinely copes with a missing husband, makes do with an absent father, and lives with unfair congregational expectations. If that's how she's feeling, I need to know, so I can make some changes.

Such feedback helps me make important decisions. At one point, I was tempted to leave our present church for another. I wasn't feeling particularly successful at the church, and weathering the storm seemed daunting. I had received an attractive offer from a much larger, more well-known congregation.

I asked Nancy if she wanted to make the move.

"No," she replied. "I wouldn't feel comfortable with the expectations of such a high-profile ministry."

Her view played a large role in my decision to stay put.

The process also applies to my children.

After I published my first book, I asked my son, "Would you like me to write another book?"

He paused and then asked, "Will it take as long as the last one?"

"Yes," I replied. "It will probably take several months to write."

"Naw," he finally said. "When you write, you never play with me."

I thanked him for his honesty, but his comment hit me hard. I thought I had done a terrific job of juggling church, family, and writing. I had crammed the whole thing into three months. But my kids see life differently, as I had to be reminded. Eventually, I decided to put the project aside for awhile. As much as I enjoy it, I don't want to write at the cost of my son saying as an adult, "Yeah, but he never played ball with me."

Doing the Unthinkable

While growing up, two of my friends were pastors' kids. One loved what his dad did for a living; the other hated it.

Why such a difference?

My disillusioned friend put it this way: "My dad always cancels me for the church." If a pastoral emergency arose just before a promised fishing trip, his father put the fishing poles back in the garage. If someone died while the car was packed for vacation, the vacation was delayed or canceled, with no compensation time given to the family. Church always came first.

The boy's father never thought to say, "I'm sorry, as important as this meeting is, I have a more important appointment with my son. You'll have to finish without me."

I'm not advocating we cancel every church appointment that conflicts with family, but spouses and children do need to feel they are priorities. Sometimes we need to cancel ministry for family. It doesn't have to be often. A few symbolic gestures go a long way. For the golfer, all it takes is one birdie to forget all the bogies on the score card. In the same way for my family, occasionally canceling a church appointment to be at a ball game or school play speaks volumes about their importance to me.

My own father modeled this principle. A public school administrator with the potential to become district superintendent, he chose to limit his career in order to spend more time with us. Instead of climbing as high as he could, he stopped when he graduated to elementary school principal. His decision freed him up to be home evenings and so to play a major role in his children's lives. It's one of the main reasons we not only loved him as our father but also followed him as our model.

The Tough Side of Success

Ironically, to our families, success may pose a greater threat than failure. Families tend to rally around each other during adversity. But success can do the reverse — it propels the successful one into wider and wider orbits of influence, often leaving the spouse and children marooned on the surface below.

Elsewhere in this book, Knute Larson comments about the price of success: "I've worked hard all my life to get to the place where I can work hard." We, too, can work hard to achieve success only to find we have to work harder once it's achieved. It's not easy stepping off the success elevator. But we must, because the greater our success, the more demands and opportunities pull at us. And the harder they pull, the more difficult it is to carve out the time the family needs. Here are three ways I combat that tension.

● *Wear your heart on your sleeve.* A few years ago, our family found itself trapped in crisis. I was preoccupied — or obsessed — for nearly a year with the moment-to-moment concern about a crisis building program. Having suddenly lost our lease, we faced the real possibility of having nowhere to meet.

The local schools were booked up, we were short on cash, and the city was breathing down our necks. Locked in the hub of crisis management, I didn't have time even to assemble a building committee. I functioned as pastor, developer, and general contractor.

With the church's future hanging in the balance, I was uptight, sometimes discouraged, despondent, and worn out. But I didn't try to hide it from the family. I wanted my children to see the downside of life as well as its upside. My family needed to accept that the church — and consequently their husband and dad — was facing a crisis of serious proportions. Life wasn't business as usual. I want to prepare them so they're not unduly disappointed or disillusioned by the hard knocks of life.

Though I didn't spare my children pain, I did help them avoid an overdose of misery.

During that dark year, every so often I'd call a halt to my preoccupation and for a brief time zero in on my kids. I surprised them by pulling them out of school to see a ball game or by going to a father/son or father/daughter weekend at a retreat center. In the midst of the crisis, I tried to communicate to each of them: "Things are hard right now, but I haven't forgotten you. I still love you."

● *Pass up some great opportunities.* Recently, having foolishly said yes to too many good offers, I was frazzled. After an exhausting trip to the Midwest, I slumped down in my favorite chair and asked my wife, "Did the kids miss me?"

"Not really," she replied. "You've been gone so much this last month, they've stopped noticing."

Craaack! I had just been whacked alongside the head with a baseball bat. But she was right. When opportunity knocks, I can find every excuse to answer the door, and consequently my priorities can get waylaid. I find it hard to pass on a great opportunity simply to remain a good dad and husband. But I must.

Learning to pass up some opportunities is a discipline I've had to develop over the years, and I'm still learning.

● *Remember what's important.* When ministry is succeeding, it's easy for the family to get caught up in the euphoria. While we ought to enjoy the prosperity God grants us, we need to guard our family identity so it doesn't become too wrapped up in the church.

My wife seems to be on top of this temptation. She cares about my work, but her feelings don't skyrocket or plummet with the offering receipts or attendance graphs. During one of the most difficult periods of my entire career, she'd often jolt me out of my introspection, saying, "We made the mortgage payment, didn't we?" or "All the kids are healthy, aren't they?"

Children are another matter, however. They run a greater risk of identifying too closely with my ministry. Our church has enjoyed a season of growth recently, and invariably on the way home from church, one of my children will ask, "How many were there today, Dad?"

"Numbers don't really matter, Son. I'm more concerned about people's spiritual growth," I usually reply — though they've obviously picked up that I'm pretty dedicated to church growth. So my caution rarely stops my son; he'll peek at the attendance book later on and then say, "Dad, how does that compare with last Sunday?" It's not only me but my family that has to work on keeping Christ, not the church, at the center.

Resentment Busters

Prevention is nice but it doesn't always work. Resentment toward ministry can seep into the chemistry of any pastor's home. Here are three antidotes that help restore my family's attitude when I sense my ministry is poisoning their souls.

• *Stop griping.* People in all walks of life complain about their work. I've listened to those in the construction business gripe about the ebb and flow of the economy, the pressure to get bids in, and the long hours. Others who hold high-profile business jobs complain of the enormous stress of fast-paced urban living.

Nearly every vocational group believes they're in a high-risk profession that threatens the ties of family. Maybe all of us are right: work is part of the curse. But I've decided to make the best of it, and Lord willing, not instill corrosive attitudes about work in my children.

So instead of complaining about ministry, I frequently remind them how fortunate I am to have a job. And I'll point out how my flexible schedule allows me to attend their Little League games when other dads cannot. When someone offers us tickets to a game or invites us to a special event, I note that these privileges are part of the perks of ministry.

• *Let them do what they want to do.* Though my wife shuns public speaking, she's perfectly suited to a ministry of hospitality, even to large numbers. She thrives on hosting large groups in our home, from welcome desserts to pastor's classes. Some months we'll have three hundred or more people pass through our home.

So while I'm quick to protect her from expectations that would put her in an uncomfortable or awkward position, I'm just as eager to turn the spotlight on her strengths, encouraging her involvement in areas where she flourishes.

● *Be at home what you are at church.* While growing up, I noticed that many of the troubled pastors' kids were those living with hypocrisy at home. At church, their fathers might have gotten rave reviews, but at home their tempers drew rage reviews. Gentleness, patience, forgiveness at church; anger, humiliation, and shame at home. Their fathers' double lives crushed their spirits. As a result, some of my friends grew up with the cynical attitude: "If people only knew. . . ."

I work hard to align my private behavior with who I am at church. Just as I confess my shortcomings to other believers, I apologize to my wife and children when I make mistakes or disappoint them or blowup. More than anything else, I want to be genuine. And I'm always amazed how well that "sells," not only in the pulpit but at home too.

You Made the Choice

Paul advised members of the Corinthian church to remain single in order to devote themselves entirely to the Lord. He observed that married individuals naturally have divided interests. He didn't say to the married, "Undivide your interests. Forget about your wife and family, and devote yourself exclusively to the Lord's work." Instead, he encouraged singles to stay single so they could give maximum time to the church.

But those of us who are married already have made the choice. We need to recognize what Scripture recognizes — in calling us to get married, God called us to divide our time and energy between home and ministry.

Devoting less time to ministry in order to attend to my family, then, is not only okay but expected by God. Since realizing this, I've felt more at peace about the time I spend with family, especially when I'm tempted to feel guilty because I'm skipping a meeting at church or putting less time into sermon preparation.

William Carey, the "Father of Modern Missions" and missionary to India, was a successful leader who chose to marry, but he couldn't bring himself to divide his interests. His family paid dearly.

One day Carey, at the time a cobbler and schoolteacher in rural England, suddenly announced he had volunteered to become a missionary to India. His wife, Dorothy, having not been consulted, refused to go with him. Carey was so intent on ministry, he decided to leave his pregnant wife and two small children and take their oldest boy with him, though he planned to retrieve the rest of his family later. Before the ship could depart, he succeeded in talking his wife into joining him immediately.

But in India, she was miserable. While he tried to get his ministry up and running, she was neglected. She became increasingly ill and his children unmanageable. Eventually Dorothy became mentally ill, and only the parental care of another missionary couple brought the children into line.

This is not to disparage Carey's ministry — he did remarkable things for the history of missions. But he wasn't a model husband and father. It's a stern reminder to me that in marrying, I chose to divide my interests, time, and energy. That means, at times, my ministry will suffer for the sake of family; at other times, family will suffer for the sake of ministry. Neither will be all it could be alone.

But it also means that at life's end, with God's help, I will be considered a success at both.

*If we're going to weather a tempest, let it be because we're
sailing in a mighty ocean rather than in a teapot.*
— *Stuart Briscoe*

CHAPTER EIGHT

The Price
of Progress

Fifteen years ago Elmbrook Church constructed a larger building
on a new site. Everyone was excited about it — well, almost
everyone.

One leader and his wife, both of whom had worked hard in
the church for years, were especially troubled. At one board meeting
during the planning stages, the man said, "When my board term is up
at the end of this year, my wife and I will be leaving the church. We will
not have any part in building a monument to Stuart Briscoe."

His comment stung, especially since I had spent a lot of time helping his wife develop a ministry in our church. But the building project had to proceed. Our old, cramped facilities severely stifled our ability to minister. Our only choices were to stay put and plateau or build and reach out.

"For everything you gain," said Emerson, "you lose something." The board member and his wife did leave the church. I felt the weight of Emerson's dictum.

When a church undertakes a building program, adds another service, or changes the style of worship music, it often loses something in the process. Just as store owners who expand their facilities pay the price in construction costs, dust, and inconvenience (as well as temporary decline in sales), so progressive churches face the possibility of lost members, lost money, and lost momentum.

Sometimes the potential gain doesn't justify the loss; other times it virtually demands it. By what criteria should we weigh the decision to venture forward? What personal temptations lurk in the process?

Personal Potholes in the Road to Progress

For many years, the music program was not a priority at Elmbrook. Eventually, people started commenting, "Why don't you get a good music pastor and build up the program here?"

When we finally hired someone, we explored together a philosophy of music ministry. Early on we realized music provided an opportunity to teach one of our fundamental values: unity in diversity and diversity in unity. Consequently, we felt the church's music should express a variety of musical tastes and styles.

In a survey, we asked the congregation what styles of music were appropriate for worship, giving various categories to choose from, as well as the all inclusive, "all of the above." In terms of broad categories, it turned out that roughly 20 percent preferred only traditional music, 20 percent only contemporary, and 60 percent "all of the above."

I showed these numbers to my daughter, Judy, who was at the time working on her Ph.D., doing statistical analysis among other things. She took one look at the numbers and said, "You've got problems."

"What do you mean?" I replied. "We've got 60 percent who want 'all of the above.' The majority will be pleased with anything we do."

"The majority doesn't matter," she said. "You won't hear from that big middle group. But you've got two groups of 20 percent opposed to each other — you're going to hear from them."

Recognizing the price we might have to pay, we still hired a keyboard player, a phenomenal talent who can perform flawlessly a stately Bach fugue or contemporary rock. We began using a synthesizer three times a month and the organ once a month.

The organist, who is talented but can play only one style well, wasn't happy and eventually left the church.

That change became the focus of controversy. People began to take sides with either the organist or keyboardist. So we called a special congregational meeting. We answered heated questions like "How come we never sing hymns anymore?" The music pastor read from a computer printout of song services in recent months, listing in detail every hymn we had sung. And once again we explained our philosophy of ministry and of music, that we are committed to unity in diversity and diversity in unity.

In the end we had to say, "We're going to continue with the approach we've taken." As a result, some people, primarily traditionalists, left the church, though we didn't suffer serious losses.

I have found that situations like this abound with temptations. Here are four.

● *To put progress over people.* We can be so committed to our vision that we lose sight of individuals. We were concerned about the organist, and we tried to find ways of including her in our expanding music ministry. But unfortunately she was hurt and did not wish to continue under the revised arrangement.

● *To have an infallibility complex.* During the music controversy, someone asked me, "Why do we Christians argue about music so much and theology so rarely?"

"Because we have a Bible for theology," I replied, "but we don't have a Bible for music. There is nothing to turn to as the final, infallible authority on music. Music is in many ways a matter of taste, which can be learned and unlearned."

And yet how tempting it is to become dogmatic about our conclusions. It's even more tempting when you're the leader and you've made a decision that isn't popular; as criticism mounts, we're tempted to see even the choice of music styles as the fault line between good and evil.

So I remind myself that on issues like music — and on any matter about which the Bible is ambiguous — that my opinion is just that. Furthermore, in virtually every change we have tried to implement at Elmbrook, people are encouraged to give feedback and suggestions so that my ideas get needed correction and balance.

● *To hide behind principle.* In several church controversies, I've heard someone claim they must follow a certain course because "It's a matter of principle!"

"Tell me," I respond, "what exactly is the principle?"

Quite often, they cannot say. So I point out, "I don't think that's a principle. I think it's a preference." A few times I've been so bold as to gently say that it's not a principle, it's a prejudice, something they've prejudged. We've all been guilty of that from time to time.

● *To seek peace at the expense of priority.* If pastors have a weakness, it is this: we're anxious to please — it's a trait that goes hand in hand with caring for people. Sometimes we're so committed to peace, we back away from new programs, even if we know they are essential for the future ministry of the church.

Knowing that the dialogue over music styles might occasionally prove as harmonious as tomcats howling at midnight, I was tempted to leave things be, stick with the traditional organ and choir, and try to make them the best possible. I'm thankful now that I didn't let this natural hesitancy rule the day.

Cost Analysis

Good questions posed before beginning a new program are inexpensive insurance. I ask myself at least three cost questions before I venture forth.

● *Will this distract us from our primary mission?* I came to Elm-brook Church fresh from ministry in Europe to countercultural youth. I was making a transition from parachurch ministry to the unchurched to pastoral ministry to the thoroughly churched. It didn't take long for the two worlds to collide.

Shortly after my arrival, I discovered that one hundred young people, most of whom had dropped out of "organized religion," were meeting at the home of one of our members. The prospect of working with them was irresistible, so I promptly went over and introduced myself. I felt at home with them immediately.

After we had gotten acquainted, I asked them, "Why aren't you in our church?"

"We've gotten the message we're not welcome," one young man replied.

"Well, you're absolutely welcome," I said. "Not only are you welcome, it's imperative you come at once. You need to belong to a fellowship of believers, and we need your drive and enthusiasm."

It took two weeks to talk them into a test ride, but they showed up one Sunday morning, adorned in tee-shirts and blue jeans. One had an American flag sewed to the seat pocket of her pants. Others wore oversized crosses that looked as if they had been pilfered from an archbishop.

The congregation reacted, to put it mildly, with consternation. A leading member of the congregation soon visited me.

"Stuart, we know that it is at your invitation these young people have come into our church," he said. "That's certainly commendable. But there's something you have to understand."

He paused momentarily, as if to gather the courage to make his main point. "Many of us have worked hard to get our own teenagers away from the influence of such kids. If you insist on bringing them here, they must be kept totally separate from our young people. Do you understand?"

"Of course, I understand," I replied. "The policy you're suggesting is similar to the one they have in South Africa. It's called apartheid." The man blinked at me in surprise.

"And it's based on fear and prejudice," I continued. "I understand those emotions because I struggle with them myself. But they have absolutely no place in the community of believers. I'm committed in this church to this kind of diversity."

An animated discussion took place between us for the next several minutes. To his credit, he listened as I explained why I had left itinerant ministry for local church ministry. "Only the church," I emphasized, "can bring together the most unlikely people into one group with other unlikely people. God is building an alternate society in a fractured world. While contemporary society builds barricades, the church ought to be building bridges. If we can achieve that, we gain a credibility no other group in society possesses."

The man then said, "I can see I'm not going to change your mind."

"No, you're not," I replied.

"Well then, let's do something about it," he said. "I propose we begin a special Sunday school class entitled 'The Generation Bridge.' Many parents like myself are struggling with a generation gap. Let's address this problem in a positive way. Let's put together a special class by invitation only and invite people from across the spectrum. We'll study the Book of James together, dividing the teaching responsibility between one older and one younger person."

I stood there astonished. It was a marvelous idea. I readily agreed, and he walked away determined to get started on the class at once.

In only a few weeks, the class began and was so successful that by the second quarter we had a waiting list to join the class.

Later in the year, I was surprised when several members of the group said, "You don't need to continue this class."

"Why?" I asked.

"Because the issues have been resolved."

The young people from outside the church had begun asking

the adults to help them understand their parents. And many of the adults had begun seeking the advice of the young people on how they might become reconciled to their estranged teenagers.

This situation could have been very costly during what was still a young pastorate. I was willing to pay those costs (potential lost members and lost credibility) for the counter-culture youth because they were, in fact, central to my mission at Elmbrook.

● *How much turmoil will this cause?* The lower the priority of the issue, the more important this question becomes, not because we lack conviction but because we "make every effort to keep the unity of the Spirit through the bond of peace" (Eph. 4:3). If we're going to weather a tempest, let it be because we're sailing in a mighty ocean rather than in a teapot. Turmoil can jeopardize everything we are striving toward, but sometimes it's worth it.

Many years ago, as the church grew rapidly, we needed to create small group opportunities. But people said they couldn't give another weekday evening in addition to Wednesday, the traditional evening for our prayer meeting. We looked at the numbers attending the Wednesday meeting, evaluated what they were doing, and decided to substitute small groups on Wednesday evening for this traditional service.

Some people, who never attended the Wednesday evening service, were horrified and said, "We've always had a Wednesday evening service."

I told them, "I didn't realize you knew!"

They vowed to leave the church, but in the end never did. Our groups have prospered so much that six new churches have been born, thanks to them.

● *Who are we choosing to lose?* With every decision we make, we lose someone, either someone now in the church or someone who might have joined in the future. The question isn't whether we will lose people, but who.

In our music controversy, I felt that if we didn't broaden the music styles, we would lose unchurched people: they might visit our church once and not return because the music was too alien. By broadening our musical styles, we implicitly "chose" to lose those adamantly committed to traditional organ and hymns, although in fact few actually departed — a credit to their grace and the quality of our music ministry.

When the Price Is Too High

Our church constitution requires that our council of elders be comprised of at least twelve male members. One by one, several younger women discovering that bylaw told me, "I won't attend a church that holds such a chauvinistic position."

The pastoral staff decided to study the issue, and after several months of research and discussion, they concluded that women could serve as members of the elder board.

The pastoral staff then presented their findings to the elder board, asking them to vote on proposing to the congregation that the congregation study the issue.

As always, we informed the congregation what the elder board was discussing. Before the elder board was to vote, we invited people to share their opinions at two meetings. Fifty people came to voice their opinions, nearly all of them opposed to the idea. Many were heated up about it and threatened, "If you make this change, we will leave the church, and we know others who will as well."

I went to some church stalwarts who were threatening to leave and said, "If you choose to leave, I'll be sorry to see you go, but I won't worry about it too much. You'll be all right, and you'll be an asset wherever you go. I'm more concerned about the women we won't reach because of our policy. They're not going to church anywhere."

When the elder council voted, seven were for a congregational study of the matter, and six were opposed. Though the measure had passed, the council was essentially divided.

In the days following the vote, I talked to the women who would be obvious choices for elder, if the measure ever went that far. Each said, "It's not worth pursuing. We've got more than enough to do already. We don't want to see people getting all upset over it." In addition, they felt good about our church's including women on the pastoral staff and the board of deacons.

In the end, even though the board had voted to pursue the

study, those who had submitted the idea decided to drop it. Though we knew younger women would continue to balk, the congregational price was too high to continue. Besides, the majority of our women were satisfied.

Cost Containment

Just as aircraft crews follow safety guidelines to minimize the risk of air travel, we do five things at Elmbrook Church to keep volatile issues from sending us into a tailspin.

● *Teach people to handle tension.* Someone has said that tension is the balance between equally valid points of view, and conflict is what comes from losing that balance. I encourage people to maintain the tension, to seek balance. I remind people that, especially in a church that values unity in diversity, there's give and take.

That isn't natural for people. There is a strong pull toward simple black-and-white, right-and-wrong answers. I have to coach the congregation every time a controversial issue arises.

● *Work with a plurality of leaders.* Decisions about controversial issues are best made within the safety of a group's wisdom.

I am the senior pastor of a multiple staff, and I'm an elder working with other elders. I would not want to be in a situation where a team atmosphere didn't exist. While working with others can be frustrating, I find comfort and safety in it. A proposal has much more credibility when presented to the congregation by a group of leaders than by one leader.

Our council of elders operates by consensus, though not unanimity. On some issues we don't take a formal vote. After discussion, the chairman may say, "My reading is that we should go ahead with this. Is that a problem for anybody?" If everyone is quiet, we do it.

● *Keep communication going both ways.* One man recently came to my office concerned about our church's stance toward Operation Rescue.

"Pastor, I heard that you and most of the elders are pro-choice."

"That's news to me," I responded. And then I assured him that none of us would commit to a position accepting abortion on demand. "In fact, we've led the church in active pro-life ministries for at least fifteen years."

By the time our meeting was over, we were laughing about the whole thing.

I assume information will get twisted. I can't say something just once and presume everyone has got it. I have to repeat important information over and over, listen to how people are hearing me, and then correct the misinformation.

One system in our church that helps us stay in touch with people's perceptions is our annual membership renewal. Each year people are asked to sign a card indicating their willingness to be committed to our church. If a member does not renew, a church leader visits them to find out why. These meetings often turn up misinformation and misunderstandings so that problems don't fester.

● *Give people time to mull it over.* A congregation may need a year to digest a major undertaking. The first reaction most people have to change is as negative as the evening news. Then after they've had time to process an idea emotionally, they may convert to a positive attitude.

When we built our new sanctuary about seventeen years ago, we completely overlooked the possibility of putting a cross at the front. After the inaugural service, a woman said she thought the lack of a cross was "disgusting." Without suggesting an oversight on our part, I simply pointed out that Jesus was not on the cross but risen.

"If you look behind the platform," I added, "you will see the baptistery, which looks like an empty tomb."

She thought that was wonderful and went away happy. I went away feeling just a tad guilty!

Not all controversy can or should be handled that easily. No matter how committed or excited we are about an idea, we shouldn't rush in where angels fear to tread. We need to count the cost, anticipate the temptations, and set up safety systems for decision making. When that has been done, and a new venture seems the way to go, boldness is the order of the day, and may the angels go with us!

PART 3

The Ups and Downs

Church work isn't war, but defeats are.
                                          — Knute Larson

CHAPTER NINE
Defeat and Disappointment

I heard it through the grapevine: twenty-three members, pained at the changes I had made during my first days at The Chapel, had secretly met to pool their frustrations.

I immediately called the de facto leader and asked for a meeting. He said he had a list of what the group had prayed (and complained) about.

"Let's get all the concerned people together," I suggested. He agreed but wanted to meet with the trustees, not me. I contended the grievances were with me, rehearsed the clear guidelines of

Matthew 18:15–17, and we agreed to convene.

I also invited all the trustees and other leaders. We had scheduled the meeting in the Fellowship Hall, and as I stepped in I was hoping it would live up to its name. But frankly, it already felt like a no-win, no-way situation.

The critical group fired away. I listened carefully to their concerns — some fair, some unfair (from my vantage of total objectivity!). A few of the complaints related to music, the way I closed my sermons and appealed to people to come to Christ, and some program changes. I neither argued nor made promises but clarified their points, some of which were based on misinformation or rumors.

Four hours later, I emerged from that meeting a little shell shocked, more aware than ever of my vulnerability as a leader.

Defeats and disappointments should not surprise us, but they usually do. My regular aches have resulted from bad sermons — especially when I knew it during the first service and dreaded having to preach it again at a couple more — or counseling that wasn't heeded or was refused.

More painful are the defeats of rejection, when people leave the church because, they say, "We're not getting fed." Or when a major program idea bombs (sometimes even with your wife). Or when a spreading rumor is increasingly believed and can't be stopped. Or when you try over and over to unite with a staff member, only to have him leave, making disparaging, and untrue, remarks upon his departure.

I often say I've been blessed with the two nicest daughters and the greatest wife, and I've pastored two terrific, balanced churches. But sometimes those gracious gifts from my Father fade into the background when I'm trying to figure out how to avoid or cope with defeat and disappointment.

Prevent Defense

People are hard work. I know because I'm one of them. Crowds can be cruel — at a soccer game or a church business meeting. When two or three are gathered together, Christ is not always in the midst of them, because sometimes they have gathered to criticize or to complain selfishly.

Before I talk about analyzing and handling defeats, let me mention two keys to preventing future defeats.

● *Don't expect most people to share the vision.* One of my greatest frustrations has been getting lay leaders to share my vision for the church. I'd often find myself agitated that I was the one always promoting, pulling, dragging, and educating to bring them up to speed on church vision.

Then one day it hit me: Don spent fifty or sixty hours a week farming, David spent fifty hours a week teaching college and administering, and Robert spent fifty hours a week running a small computer business. But I spend my waking hours each week thinking about church. No wonder these men can't match my enthusiasm, passion, and vision for ministry. I'm being paid to think about these things full time.

I've since concluded that people won't have as much vision in areas where they haven't invested much time. I'm visionless when it comes to my car or my money. Even lay leaders who get excited about their specific contributions to the church often can see only the narrow vision of their specific ministry. A person with a passion for evangelism might say, "The church ought to be about winning souls," and fail to see the value of other ministries.

Today, in contrast to twenty years ago, those who invest the energy to attend church do it because they want to, not because they have to. Most want their church to succeed. We shouldn't, though, assume that people will automatically catch our vision for the church.

Keeping that vision alive and making it happen is the pastor's responsibility. Though vision needs to be shared and owned by other leaders and communicated with the whole church, it's our initiative that keeps dreams alive. Of all the leaders in the church, only I will wake up in the middle of the night with another solution for a church problem. Even my wife can wait until breakfast to hear it.

● *Don't take votes that won't pass.* At the time I thought he was a chicken, afraid of making the hard decision. Now I know he was wise.

He was the pastor I worked with in my first two years of ministry. "Let's pray about this decision and vote on it next month," he'd often say about decisions teetering precariously at a board meeting. His wise counsel, which I've since employed liberally, has become my common practice.

I put off decisions even when I'm pretty confident I could at the moment sway people sitting on the fence. I'd rather just pray, or talk with them one-to-one than pressure them on the spot. I don't want to take a vote unless I'm sure it will pass.

Even city councils — or Congress — do not vote on bills at their first reading. Senators and representatives and trustees and deacons and staff hate surprises, resist change (at least until they feel comfortable), and need time to process new ideas.

Introduce it, let it leak, reintroduce it, get more input, let others alter and own the idea (especially the Baby Boomers), and generally seek to make it a team effort. Lone Rangers lose.

The Turmoil and Its Temptations

Church work isn't war, but defeats are. No one likes to lose, especially we pastors who eat and sleep the local church. When I face a loss, I have to process a surge of emotions, none of which feels like much fun.

Certainly disappointment tops the list, like the time an alternative worship service at The Chapel struck out. The night we launched "Saturday at Six," a service designed for the unchurched, 670 people showed up. The staff and I were thrilled; the future looked bright. Several months later, however, attendance had tapered off, and by the time we buried the service, only seventy people were showing up.

Anger and fear are other opponents to face after a loss. Both battered me when we recently called the police on one of our part-time interns for allegedly sexually molesting several of our junior high boys. On his application he had lied about his past, so he had sneaked through our hiring gates. And though he had worked only three months at The Chapel, the news of this tragedy made it to the media (which, by the way, treated us fairly).

I was angry at the potentially sustained hurt inflicted on these boys, angry that this person had slipped through our security, angry at myself that it had happened under my watch as pastor. Anger gave way to fear when it struck me that it could happen again.

Naturally, discouragement can also set in. Several years ago, I invested much of myself into an alcoholic whose life was collapsing around him. I was the messianic pastor on a mission to save this man from his "demon of drink," as he called it. We had a pattern to our relationship: I'd receive from him a blubbering phone call, go pick him up from a local bar, and then drive him home, trying to convince him that his lifestyle was dumb and that there was yet hope for him.

Once when he called me from the bar, too drunk to drive, I refused to pick him up.

"Jed," I said, "I can't help you. I haven't helped you yet, and I'm not coming tonight; I'm staying in bed."

Jed exploded into anger and slammed down the phone. A few days later, he was drunk again. This time he got a taxi and asked to be driven to my house. On the way over to my place, Jed told the taxi driver his plans to kill me. Fortunately neither my wife nor I was home. (The driver happened to be a casual member of our church, and as he told me this quaint story a few weeks later, I asked him the obvious question: "Why in the world did you drive him to my house?" He hadn't thought of that!)

A few years later in his late thirties, Jed died of an alcohol-related illness. His continuing addiction and eventual death were a personal letdown. I felt discouraged that all my efforts were in vain, that perhaps I could have done or said more or convinced him to see a professional.

Of course I know better than to take these things personally (except the part about wanting to kill me — I always get offended by such lack of diplomacy). But what I know and what I feel are not always aligned.

Lamenting such a loss, however, is healthy. When we love our people, we're not simply going to shrug our shoulders after a disappointment. But ultimately I know that everyone does exactly what he or she wants to do, no matter what I say or try, and I must carry my own burden, not theirs.

We're also tempted to get revenge, to manipulate people. I've heard of embattled pastors saying, "If we don't make this program a priority, I'm leaving" or "If this doesn't happen in two years, I'll resign."

Another tactic is to make people feel guilty by our open self-pity, wearing our emotions on our shirt-sleeves or publicly lamenting the defeat.

Defeat is tough, but we make things tougher if we let emotions like these undermine our ministries.

Anatomy of Defeats

Rather than wallowing in defeats, I try to analyze them; that helps me get up after being down. It not only softens the emotional pain of defeats, it also helps me feel somewhat in control, as I see what went wrong and how I can do things differently in the future.

Sometimes defeat is a result of my not leading hard enough. We recently began raising money for another capital investment. When we did this five years earlier, we successfully raised $3.5 million over three years, and on the last Sunday of the campaign, we took in $159,000, the exact amount needed to burn our mortgage. Among the many calculated steps the leadership took to raise the money, a team of volunteers visited every member in our congregation, explaining the need and asking for help.

So we wanted to raise $3.5 million for the new campaign, as well. However, we skipped several important steps before launching the fund drive. Some were saying to me, "Don't worry. We don't need to visit every person again; we'll easily raise the money." So I backed off from demanding we repeat each step that contributed to our past success. And the church paid for it; we fell slightly short of our goal.

Other times, an early negative vote or thumbs down on a project often points to a dearth of research and development. If I can't create a chart or describe in detail the program I'm selling, saying, "This is why I think we should start this ministry (or build this facility, or whatever), and here are the needs it meets," then I need to go back to the drawing board. Or if I'm the only one who believes in or banks on a proposal, I know the proposal — submitted at whatever level — is premature.

The way our trustee board is structured now, few if any decisions are made at the board level that aren't first proposed by a smaller group of four or five board members. That ensures that a specific issue — whether about finances, property, or missions — is thoroughly researched before the proposal goes to the floor.

Often pastors or church leaders present ideas that are defeated because ideas are sprung on the church, catching many by surprise. Then if we go down in a trail of smoke, it's not so much because of opposing convictions but shock. People hate surprises.

After several years at The Chapel, I wanted to hire an executive pastor (a "director of ministries," as we choose to call the position) to oversee the ministry to staff; up until then I had performed that function.

I gradually leaked the idea to the staff but received a cool response. Few were thrilled at the prospect of another boss; by this time, most of the staff were acclimated to my style of leadership.

Recognizing trouble, I backed off from my initial proposal and waited two years before I broached the subject again. During the interim, I set about to educate and inform the staff, allowing them to express their concerns and to *feel* the need for a change. Later most of them favored the addition, and it has worked well.

In some cases, though, what seems like a defeat is simply a necessary loss. Sometimes it's a case of personality conflict. An Arizona pastor tried everything he could to salvage a staff relationship. The detractor quibbled and bickered with the leadership style of the pastor, and in the process disrupted the unity of the other pastors on staff.

The senior pastor tried three ways to resolve the tension. Finally both the senior pastor and the staff member punted, saying, "This isn't working out. One of us has to leave." It wasn't the senior pastor.

Sometimes we lose members for no other reason than an honest difference of opinion. One woman who met with me to air her complaints said, "I don't think I can continue to attend this church. People laugh too much in the services, and I don't believe laughter should be a part of worshiping God." I spent the next hour with her, listening and explaining our church personality and my own convictions.

It was a waste of time. Neither she nor I was planning to change. Neither of us laughed when she left.

Graceful Defeats

Analysis gives only so much comfort. We still have to live with the reality that, for whatever reason, our ministry has suffered a setback. Sometimes the difference between a professional and a rookie is the grace with which they handle defeats. Here are a few lessons I've learned about that.

● *Get up.* Mike Singletary, former linebacker for the Chicago Bears, was famous for initially getting blocked out of a play but still making the tackle. What happened after he got knocked down on the first block?

He got up.

There's a lot to say for good old-fashioned grit. It's probably healthy to take five minutes a day to worry and then get up and do something else.

● *Switch to something fun.* The world has not ended with any of the defeats I have endured. So one helpful practice is to go play. For me that usually means basketball or jogging or a walk with my wife or a few minutes of sports talk or joking with somebody. Breaks are a big help and certainly intended by God for our mental health.

Some of the staff plays basketball on Fridays at four. It's a great way to end the regular office hours. It's a time to lay aside defeats or challenges and become kids again, buffeting the body and sweating like nothing else matters.

● *Come at it from another angle.* In my first church, we sported an official board of twenty-eight members, many of whom were elected by default — for example, the head usher and Sunday school superintendent were automatically board members by virtue of their offices.

I suggested several changes to the cumbersome board but was rebuffed. I then decided to take another tack. First, I prayed for the opportunity to make the changes and then went about studying biblical leadership with the board and other, unofficial leaders of the church.

Second, I started meeting regularly with the six-man deacon board, instilling my vision in them for the future direction of the church.

Over time these men grew into an informal cabinet of advisers, often taking the lead and proposing items to the official board. Several years later, after preaching on the subject and holding question-and-answer "press conferences," the congregation voted to change the constitution and move to a smaller board of pastors and lay elders.

● *Find a shoulder to cry on.* While I reveal most things to my wife — especially in the area of personal hurt — I don't always tell her my latest defeat at church. I don't want her to feel negative towards anyone, especially when letdowns are part of the normal routine of ministry.

So I share some of my frustrations with others. One of those persons is a man on staff with whom I can laugh as well as share my pain. Other times, it's a pastor-friend with whom I've been meeting for twenty-five years. Sometimes I just need to talk through the defeat or vent some frustration.

Actually, God has been so good to me that at times, after sharing a concern with my friend, I will say, "Remind me not to take The Chapel for granted and to give God the credit."

The worst defeat would be to forget who gives "every good and perfect gift." Sometimes a defeat, when contrasted with other parts of my life, seems so insignificant. Rereading the grouchy letter and forgetting the four positive letters and three thank-you notes is so easy. I've learned my glass is always half full — not half-empty — and often even nine-tenths full!

Better Defeat than Safety

Before I close this chapter, I must clarify that my relationships in my two churches have been just plain wonderful. Most things turned down or delayed by the approving board were done for good reason — I can see in retrospect.

But just as every missed shot in basketball is a defeat of sorts, so is the rebuffing of any of our plans. So every day in ministry has its setbacks or disappointments, though that says nothing about the quality of relationships between pastor and people.

The meeting I mentioned at the start of this chapter was long, tense, and painful. Still, the men, who all had good hearts (and had the normal hesitancy to accept the new pastor after a beloved and long-term predecessor), felt they had been heard. Sometimes that in itself is the biggest need. Twenty-one of the original twenty-three have become my friends; two ended up leaving the church. It turned out to be a discouragement that brought healing.

I rest in two assurances: God is sovereign, and people will do what they want to do. Those two beliefs free me from the obsession to try to control everything in my life and ministry. After I've made amends, informed and educated those around me, allowed time for ideas to gel and relationships to form, I can punt to the ultimate grace and providence of God.

And while this is easier to preach than to feel, I know I must grow through defeat and the pain it inflicts on me. Theodore Roosevelt's philosophy about risk taking, which hangs in my study, keeps me motivated through setbacks:

"It is not the critic who counts: not the man who points out how the strong man stumbled or where the doer of deeds could have done them better. The credit belongs to the man who is actually in the arena; whose face is marred by dust and sweat and blood; who strives valiantly; who errs, and comes short again and again, because there is not effort without error and shortcoming; who does actually try to do the deed; who knows the great enthusiasm, the great devotion, and spends himself in a worthy cause; who, at the worst, if he fails, at least fails while daring greatly.

"Far better it is to dare mighty things, to win glorious triumphs even though checkered by failure, than to rank with those poor spirits who neither enjoy nor suffer much because they live in the gray twilight that knows neither victory nor defeat."

Failure is the path to success, but only if we learn from mistakes and press on.

— Stuart Briscoe

CHAPTER TEN

Making the Most of Mistakes

Before I came to Elmbrook Church, a good friend said he didn't think I would last twelve months (I had no previous experience as a pastor, and I was new to America). To survive, he said, I had to avoid two things: a building program and a constitutional revision.

The first week after I assumed pastoral responsibilities, the deacons reported that the constitution was outdated and needed a revision; they had waited for my arrival to begin the process.

Bearing in mind my friend's "prophecy," I stalled for twelve months, but then we got into it. After several committee meetings without incident, one night, at a congregational meeting, I went through a cheese grater.

We were discussing the mode of baptism when some disagreements surfaced. The meeting quickly turned into a debate between me and one person after another who jumped up in the congregation. At first they addressed the issue, but as tempers frayed, they began to attack me. Someone suggested, "If you don't like it in America, it might be a good idea if you went back to England."

My wife, Jill, felt people were beating up on me, so she stood to speak in my defense. But before she could finish a sentence, she burst into tears and ran from the auditorium. A half dozen others walked out of the meeting. It was quite unpleasant.

That night I drove home with a deep sense of failure and disbelief. I had done what they asked: suggested ways to bring the constitution in line with our actual church practice. But the result had been open conflict and anger. I had gone into the meeting with somewhat naive assumptions, and when tempers began to flare, I didn't manage the conflict well.

I had previously worked as a bank examiner and, before that, had served in the Marines, but I had never been shredded as I experienced that night.

Grave concerns filled my mind. I realized I didn't know my people as I thought. Their emotional intensity shocked me. My wife felt she could never show her face again at church. I wondered if we hadn't blundered coming from Britain to America.

Slip-ups haunt every pastor: a sermon that folds to the ground like a shot mallard, annual goals that aren't reached, a meeting that runs amuck for lack of preparation. And some "slip-ups" are much more than that: shouting at a member, inattention to the budget, talking publicly about something mentioned in a pastoral conversation. These can cause long-term problems.

After twenty-two years at the same church, however, I've learned that mistakes needn't be final nor fatal.

In the Wake of a Mistake

At the time, mistakes never feel like "the kiss of Jesus," as Mother Teresa described some failures, meaning that they drive us to God and away from dependence on ourselves. Rather, our hearts churn with painful emotions and impulses. If we don't understand these emotions, we're likely to make things worse.

● *Regret:* Those who marry at our church undergo premarital counseling and take personality inventories. Sometimes, even though these precautions signal that the couple should have a successful marriage, I have nagging reservations. I can't always put my finger on what bothers me, and I wonder whether it is my place to ask the couple to wait longer.

And sometimes, three years later they're separated or divorced. Then I wonder, *Is this partly my fault? Should I have taken stronger leadership in their lives? Should I have refused to marry them?*

Second-guessing myself is easy. On occasion I find myself thinking things like, *I should have been more sensitive with her,* or *I should have guessed what was happening with him.* Usually my failings in dealing with others aren't major in themselves, but at the time they feel that way.

● *Frustration:* At one stage when we were experiencing significant growth, we realized a considerable number of people stood on the sidelines; they were not getting integrated into the church's life.

I came up with what I considered to be a marvelous plan for providing pastoral care for individuals on the fringe. The idea was to recruit leaders who would (a) commit to praying daily for designated individuals who weren't in a small group, (b) call them once a week on the phone, and (c) visit them in their homes once every quarter.

On paper, the structure looked impressive, and the more I discussed it with others in the church, the more enthusiastic they became. So we began implementing the plan.

Immediately we heard complaints. "Couldn't we just pray for these people when they come to mind?" leaders objected. Concerning the weekly phone call, "It seems a bit much," they said candidly.

Visiting everyone once a quarter drew even less enthusiasm: "Do we actually have to meet with them in their homes? What if we just seek them out after church?"

The so-called "periphery people" didn't like the scheme either. They were loathe to divulge personal, specific prayer requests. They stayed on the periphery because they felt comfortable there, content to remain believers rather than belongers.

In theory, the whole plan had sounded marvelous. In reality, no one wanted to have anything to do with it. I did my best to talk people into it but grew only more frustrated with them. Eventually I realized that the idea was faulty given the mindset of our culture. The whole enterprise finally died a quiet death and was laid to rest in a private ceremony with few mourners.

- *Self-pity:* We can adopt a victim mentality. We can feel sorry for ourselves. That's as natural as holding our hand after burning it on a hot griddle. But if it lasts very long, the wound never heals; the pain never leaves, and we are crippled. There is no doubt that some churches abuse their pastors, and I know not a few young men — some in our congregation — who have been so hurt in other churches that they feel they can never face the ministry again.

- *Paralysis:* After a failure a pastor sometimes can't snap out of it, can't move on with confidence to the next challenge. When we dwell on the past — wishing over and over that we had handled a situation differently, sliding into depression, questioning our abilities — we suffer a paralysis that only compounds our mistakes. In some ways, failure is the path to success, but only if we learn from mistakes and press on.

- *Flight reflex:* One young man in our church started a daughter church that grew rapidly. After a few years his church's leaders decided they needed a constitution. While trying to hammer out the details, the church split.

Completely discouraged, he came to see me. "Stuart, you taught us that when instituting change, we have to drop the pebble in the pool and then wait. I did that, but it didn't work." (I had told him that analogy to show that we should never try to make changes until we have dropped an idea in people's minds, given them time to think it over, get accustomed to it, and then give feedback.)

"Tell me what you did," I said. The divisive issue was the role of women. He had pressed for consensus too fast, not allowing the "ripples" enough time to work their way to the bank and back before he called for a decision. I said, "You didn't drop a pebble in the pool; you heaved a boulder into a bathtub, and it went right through the floor!"

Now he and his wife were discouraged and sure they should leave the church. "Failure isn't final," I told him. "I don't question your integrity, and neither should anyone else. Let the dust settle for a while. Admit to the people, "I made an error in judgment. Let's put this behind us.""

He stayed at the church, and now they're doing extremely well. And in recent months, we have seen major reconciliations taking place after years of estrangement.

Whose Ears Will Hear?

Years back I traveled to England to preach for several weeks. I was greatly refreshed by the fellowship with other church leaders and the ministry that occurred. By the end of my trip, I felt like a new man, and I realized how tired I had been. I thought, *The last few months, I haven't been giving my best to the congregation.*

My first Sunday home I said to the church, "Before I preach today, I want you to know I had a wonderful and refreshing time in England. It helped me see that I haven't been all that you could reasonably expect. Recently I've been resting on my oars a bit. I apologize for that."

People responded in two ways.

Some said, "Stuart, that was the greatest thing you've ever done. Now we know you're human."

Others said, "Don't ever do that again. That's totally unnerving." They didn't want their pastor taken off the pedestal.

When we make mistakes, it can be another mistake to tell others about it. Telling eager listeners may backfire. They go home and relate a slightly different version of the story to their friends.

Their friends tell other friends a different version still. In the end, it sounds like I've been sleeping in my office all day!

Since many can't handle such information, I admit mistakes on a need-to-know basis. What is the group's role? How will my admission help the hearers? How would the church be hurt if they didn't know?

As I look back on my "resting on the oars" admission, I realize the congregation didn't need to know. It made me feel better, but all the people needed was my renewed energies.

The Comeback

"Nothing is easy in war," said Dwight Eisenhower. "Mistakes are always paid for in casualties, and troops are quick to sense any blunder made by their commanders."

That accurately describes pastoral blunders, as well. Though the price of failure is steep, it is not necessarily terminal.

David's recovery from his sin with Bathsheba, referred to in Psalm 51, is a model for recovery from any serious mistake.

1. Admit the failure to yourself. "I know my transgression, and my sin is always before me" (v. 3). People try many things to avoid repairing the gushing hole in the hull that results from a grave failure: they blame others, rationalize, deny, make excuses. But if they refuse to admit their failing, they will eventually founder and sink.

2. Admit the failure to the Lord. "Against you, you only, have I sinned and done what is evil in your sight" (v. 4).

3. Claim God's faithfulness and forgiveness. "Have mercy on me, O God, according to your unfailing love; according to your great compassion blot out my transgressions" (v. 1).

4. Come to terms with your sinful humanity. "Surely I was sinful at birth, sinful from the time my mother conceived me" (v. 5). Errors can overwhelm and destroy those who have never faced up to their sinful nature.

A pastor friend told how an elderly woman in his church lay in the hospital near death. She had been seriously ill for some time, and he had seen her regularly. When one early morning he heard that her condition had become critical, he knew an immediate visit was in order. He planned to see her first thing after breakfast.

Having just faced two or three intense days, my friend was in no mood to jump into another hectic day. He dawdled over breakfast, sipping an extra cup or two of coffee while browsing the paper. When he finally arrived at the hospital ward, the woman's son was just walking out: his mother had died ten minutes earlier.

Naturally, my friend was crushed; he knew he should have been there at least for the son (the women had been unconscious the whole night). Still, my friend recognized it wasn't the first time he'd failed as a pastor, nor would it be the last. He sought God's forgiveness, vowed to be more responsive the next time, and went on with his pastoral duties, albeit sorely chastened.

5. Ask God to put you together again. "Create in me a pure heart, O God, and renew a steadfast spirit within me" (v. 10). David turns the corner and takes hold of God's pleasure in restoring the broken.

6. Turn to the task at hand. "Then I will teach transgressors your ways" (v. 13). David has dealt with his failing and restored his relationship with God; now he gets on with it. He deals with the new realities and makes the most of them.

I was listening to a football game recently and Dan Marino of the Miami Dolphins threw an interception. The commentator said, "One great strength of Marino is, like all great quarterbacks, he has a short memory." In other words, he doesn't dwell on interceptions. He knows what he did wrong. Instead of being paralyzed by an interception, he thinks, *What's the next play?*

As a fallible person, I assume I will make mistakes. But I don't spend a lot of time analyzing and regurgitating them. I learn from them and then move on.

In Case of a Moral Failure

A friend from another country called me after his moral failure came into the open. He had carried on a longstanding adulterous relationship with a woman in the congregation. The woman finally couldn't bear the guilt any longer, and she told a friend, who leaked the news to others.

My friend apologized to the congregation. He expected them to forgive, take a vote of confidence, and carry on as before. Instead they told him to leave, and now he was bitter.

He had no sense that what he had done would call for more than the mere restoring of a fallen brother. A leader had grossly abused his trust and had done so for an extended period. He didn't realize it would take an equally intense repentance and period of restoration to regain his pastoral credibility.

Spurgeon, in his *Lectures to My Students,* quoted another minister: "When a preacher of righteousness has stood in the way of sinners, he should never again open his lips in the great congregation until his repentance is as notorious as his sin." I would paraphrase that to say, he belongs on the back pew until he is as well-known for his works of grace as for the notoriety of his failure.

A minister friend of mine sinned sexually, resigned his church, and underwent denominational discipline. He complained to me, "I'm an outcast. Other pastors with whom I used to talk regularly won't have anything to do with me. I've cried all the tears I can cry. I've apologized to everyone I can. I've undergone discipline. It's as if people want to keep on punishing me. I don't think we understand grace."

I feel for this man's pain, but I would suggest that he needs to be willing not only to weep and apologize but also to do what it takes to establish credibility again. That takes time. He must accept less responsibility, less visibility, perhaps even go back to square one.

Many years ago in England, a parliamentary minister was charged with having an affair with a call girl who at the same time was having an affair with a high member of the Russian embassy. He stood in the House of Commons and denied it.

The next day, he was exposed as a liar. He immediately stood in Parliament and resigned. He left the public eye and began to work quietly for charity. Years later the queen honored him for his charitable work.

A like response to failure is fitting for any fallen pastor.

Staying the Course

In the constitutional debate that turned ugly, some older and wiser heads helped me out of hot water by coming to my side and whispering, "Why don't we adjourn the meeting and continue tomorrow night?"

I agreed. Afterward they sat down with me and advised, "Stuart, we aren't tackling this right. Instead of your standing up there taking all the shots, let's put a table up front and have a panel." They explained where the people were coming from and what kind of leadership I needed to exert in the situation.

An older woman in the congregation came to Jill, who had decided she would never set foot in church again, and said, "Jill, you will simply dry your face and come back and face the congregation tomorrow night. They love you, and they'll forgive you. In fact, your stock has probably gone up considerably because you stood up for your husband; we see that you feel deeply."

We followed their counsel. The issues weren't easily resolved in one night, but over the ensuing weeks and months, the constitution was rewritten, and the church moved forward. Twenty-two years later, I am still the pastor of Elmbrook Church, living proof that mistakes aren't final.

I've worked hard to get to the place where I can work hard.
— *Knute Larson*

When Things Are Going Well

S uccesses can be sweet — and sour.

The organ had started the prelude as would-be worshipers filed in for the third worship service. I was welcoming the people to our service at one of the doors.

I glanced at my watch; in only a minute or two I would need to make my way to the front of the sanctuary. I reached out and turned to welcome the next person.

"You're the most wonderful pastor in the world," the woman said, shaking my hand. Her husband nodded in agreement.

I smiled and turned to greet the couple standing behind them. As I reached out to shake the hand of the husband, he faked a punch to my solar plexis and said, "You're the stupidest pastor I've ever heard of." He seemed to have meant it, and his wife nodded in agreement.

I smiled again but chose to say nothing and then walked to the front of the sanctuary to begin the service. The couples had not overheard each other, but I clearly heard them both. The second couple had heard rumors about a particular staff problem at the time, and they chose to believe the worst about me.

As I tried to switch my mind and emotions to the next worship service, I asked God for grace. I concluded that if I believed either of those couples, I would be in trouble. But those sorts of comments come with the territory of outward success.

All pastors know times when things go well. We may not pastor a megachurch, but many of us pastor churches with a larger staff and budget than our previous charge. And no matter where we are, during some seasons of ministry, programs work, finances are healthy, and people are helped.

Though we may not be able to equate this outward success with God's ultimate standards, it is a reality most of us will experience. And it feels good.

No matter how it feels, though, successes, like wealth, are resources of which we need to be good stewards.

Uneasy Achievement

The day before the last presidential election, President George Bush was on top of the world; he presided over the United States of America, the world's sole military superpower. The day after, when Governor Bill Clinton won the election, President Bush was considered a loser, a "has been." He went from world leader to lame duck in a few short hours. It's a thin line.

Riding the crest of a wave is nice, but sooner or later the wave goes flat. That's threatening. That's just one downside to successes we must be prepared for. Here are some precarious aspects of success that I experience.

• *Lonely decisions.* I sat in a meeting with nine men, several of whom were CEO's of strong corporations, discussing a $3 million building campaign. We had spent months in preparation and prayer for this moment, gathering data and getting everyone's input. Now the decision to press ahead came down to this meeting. Suddenly it was silent.

Why is it so quiet? I thought. *Why doesn't somebody speak up?*

Several years removed from that evening, I can still feel the jolt that struck my heart when I realized they were waiting for my direction.

"Let's do it," I finally said. My decision was not a knee-jerk. We all had prayed and planned for months, and the decision was unanimous; everybody was enthusiastically on board.

I work hard to make leadership at The Chapel a team effort, but I know the more successes I lead us through, the more people look to me for leadership. That, at times, can feel lonely.

• *Fear of failure.* Jerry Faust, football coach at the University of Akron, recently stopped by my office to wish me well after the papers reported the news that one of our part-time interns was accused of sexual misconduct. Jerry knows about the highs and lows of success. At one time he was the winningest high school football coach in the country. He then graduated to the "big leagues," becoming head coach at the University of Notre Dame.

But Jerry's tenure was brief, punctuated by negative press coverage. His past successes did not guarantee success at Notre Dame. And neither do mine nor yours.

Most leaders of successful churches experience doubts: *Am I doing the right thing?* and *Will it work tomorrow?* Such fear, while healthy in most cases, isn't paralyzing. But it is a pressure.

• *Insecurity.* Recently a Michael Jordan jersey went on the auction block, and someone picked it up for a cool $27,000. But the jersey of the newest star of the NBA, Shaquille O'Neal, of the Orlando Magic, brought $55,000. Even the fame of Michael Jordan can't last forever; a fresher, younger face soon comes along and captures the media's attention.

That volatility in a church setting can make the successful pastor feel threatened; what worked last year may not work this year.

● *Work begetting work.* I'm not proud of this fact, but I probably work harder than any other staff person at The Chapel. And what has that gotten me? More work! I've worked hard during my twenty-six years of ministry only to get to the place where I can work hard.

I can't walk by a piece of paper lying on the church parking lot, for instance, without picking it up. I carry within me a burden for the well-being of the entire church, and that can feel overwhelming at times. When I look in the mirror, I don't say, "Boy, I am successful!" I can't ever remember such a thought. Instead I say, "I've got another challenge today."

Recently a pastor said to me, "It must be nice having a staff as big as yours." At that moment, embroiled in a staff controversy that was consuming my waking thoughts, I didn't feel so lucky. He didn't realize that leading a staff successfully doesn't take work away. In many areas of ministry, when things go well, it means more opportunities for ministry. Success breeds success. And that breeds work.

● *Less intimacy.* Not long ago I ate breakfast with a leader from a denomination. He wanted to "pick my brain" about leading a church like The Chapel. I felt uncomfortable during our breakfast because throughout our conversation he insisted on calling me "Dr. Larson."

"Please call me Knute," I said. And I repeatedly called him by his first name. As we shook hands to leave, he said, "Dr. Larson, what a privilege it has been to be with you."

Oh well.

● *The weight of responsibility.* Shortly after the revelation about the part-time intern who had been accused of molesting boys, a group of church leaders with whom I meet regularly wanted to know how I was holding up.

"We know you're not to blame," one of them said. "As the

captain of the ship, though, we suspect you're feeling some heat."

I appreciated that comment because it communicated their genuine concern for me. Yet I couldn't help but hear an underlying message: "You are the captain, and this happened on your ship during your watch."

I feel the weight of responsibility also when I realize what a difference I make in people's lives. About once or twice a month, some mother brings up her little boy who says he wants to meet me. He shakes my hand as if I'm a major league star. When I lean down and talk to him, he doesn't say anything. He just stares.

That's scary for him — and for me. He looks up to me as a model of goodness, perhaps even of God.

● *Less energy for people.* Recently my wife and I were invited over to a church member's home for pizza on a Sunday evening. Several other couples from the church would be there as well. The day of the pizza party — a Sunday — I had spoken six times. By evening I was emotionally and physically spent.

Driving over to the party, I asked my wife, "Why are we doing this?" The last thing I was ready for was two hours of small talk.

Less time for spontaneous relationships is a sacrifice of pastoral life. And as I mentioned, things are busier when things are going well. When I do carve out time for relationships outside my inner circle, I fear raising the expectations of others, who, seeing me at a dinner party of one of their friends, expect me to accept an invitation to their party.

Each week I keep a couple of appointment slots open for spontaneous meetings, and I try to have lunch once a week with a visitor. I also teach a restaurant Bible study every Tuesday morning, which is open to everyone, and I roam the halls before and after all services.

Living with Success

Successes, like all of God's gifts, are meant to be enjoyed in freedom. God put taste in food so we'd enjoy it, not just so we could tell the difference between steak and peas. He gave pleasure in marriage and sex for the joy they can bring us. Similarly, it's proper to enjoy outward pastoral successes. They give more freedom to try new ministries, more respect from our community, and more glory to God.

I've been pleasantly surprised by success. I never expected to pastor such a large church, and I'm regularly grateful for our growth in people, budget, and programs. God has been good!

Still we are wise to remember that success brings with it numerous temptations — pride, sloth, and ingratitude, to name three. Though I use a number of strategies to maintain my character, these are the most helpful.

First, as I mentioned, I keep up the pace, working as hard as ever. If you took a cross-section of national Christian leaders and attempted to identify common denominators of their success, I think you'd come up with only two: a passion to serve Christ and hard work — no matter the work involved. Methods will vary but usually not these two conditions.

Recently one of our talented but boisterous interns made his feelings known about administration: "I don't like this paper work you're giving me. I want to lead people."

I asked, "How can you lead without some administration? Impossible. See it as a way to lead."

Many tasks of even a successful ministry are not grandiose or high-powered executive privileges. They are work that simply needs doing.

Second, I try to be generous with praise. That's hard when I'm striving to work ever harder at being faithful to my calling.

On anonymous surveys I have asked the church staff to give me, I rank lowest on giving praise for things accomplished and highest on identifying dreams still to be achieved.

Okay, I accept I often forget to praise our staff enough for each year's Christmas production, for example, taking extra time to celebrate the success. (They are great!) The day following a big production I'm likely to be looking ahead to Easter. My mind naturally and immediately races to the next item on my agenda.

I'm working on this at home, too. When my wife has to say, "Wasn't that a good meal," I know I blew it. At both church and home, I'm learning the importance of stopping and saying, "Thank you" both to God and the people who have done so much to make this or that program a success.

Third, I try to stay patient. When things go well, the natural tendency is to expect more of the same, and the sooner the better. When the next success doesn't happen as quickly or shine as brightly, we're tempted to get angry at the church or move on to greener pastures.

As I mentioned earlier, after eight years of steady growth in Ashland, the first church I pastored, I still enjoyed my ministry but wanted some additional challenges. In God's grace, I was asked to be executive director of my denomination's national department of Christian education and church growth. I also did some teaching at their seminary. Much of my work I did by phone, but I also traveled once a month to the national office.

As a result I stayed an additional seven years, for a total of fifteen, at that church, and there enjoyed seeing more people come to Christ and more programs meet people's needs.

Fourth, I don't spend much time thinking about success. When I'm playing basketball, if I bask in how well I'm playing, I'll stop playing well. Instead, I think about what I'm supposed to do next: Should I set a screen? Get the ball and shoot it? Position myself for a rebound?

In ministry, I don't want to spend a lot of time thinking about what I've achieved. Instead, I want to concentrate on what I'm to do next: finish a sermon, prepare for a board meeting, listen to a secretary. If I concentrate on doing the next thing well, I'll better my chances that things will continue to go well.

Fifth, I try to remember from where I came. That is perhaps the quickest way to regain a sense of humility, a sense that God has given me any success I'm enjoying.

Looking at my upbringing and the experiences of my early years, I am indebted to the grace of God. My parents divorced when I was young, and I remember as a child once stepping between my parents when they became angry. My report cards in the third and fourth grades reflected my anxiety; they were regularly marked with the comment, "Restless, inattentive."

I lost a 14-year-old sister one Father's Day; she fell off a horse and died. My mother never got over her death, and it probably contributed to her own death a few years later, in her mid-forties.

Though I grew up in several good churches, I have painful memories of the church being not so good. When my parents waved good-bye to each other, their church waved good-bye to them. Often I experienced tight legalism and gossip-filled infighting, so much so that initially I declared I would never be a pastor.

How God used that background to give me gifts and opportunities to minister to so many people today is beyond me. It simply confirms a recent sermon I preached: "Live with a Semicolon." The semicolon statement of all of life is this: I am a sinner; I am in Christ. That is how I think about my past troubles, even my past failures; they are semicolons on the way to Christ's redemptive work in me and through me. When I remember that, success doesn't have a chance of going to my head.

Finally, I stay on my knees. Martin Luther once said that normally he spent an hour in morning prayer. But when he had an especially busy day ahead, he would spend two.

The specific numbers may not apply, but the more successful I am, the more I feel the need to be on my knees. Frankly, my passion for the Lord is harder to keep up now. I've learned over the years how to preach sermons and teach in a way that will answer people's questions. I also know how to say a prayer that's personal and yet canned. In order to prevent putting my ministry on auto-pilot, I have to work ever harder at private devotions with God. I really do want to talk to him, cry to him, express my love to him, and keep my heart warm.

The main issue is Christ. When I do walk with him, I can better seek his pleasure, relax in his sovereignty, and grow through pain and joy.

Corrie ten Boom was once asked how she handled all the

accolades of people. She said, "Well, I take the flowers, and I thank the people, and I enjoy the flowers a little bit. Then each evening, I put them in a bunch and give them back to the Lord where they belong."

That's how I ultimately want to handle my successes.

Two dangers exist for pastors when it comes to setting standards for success. One is to shoot for the moon. The other is to throw in the towel.

— *Stuart Briscoe*

CHAPTER TWELVE

Measuring Success

When I was a young businessman in England, a group of church leaders got together in a major city to plan how they could sponsor an evangelist and hold meetings.

An older gentleman, something of a self-appointed archbishop, rose to address the assembly. He gave a stirring speech decrying the idea of making plans to increase the number of believers. He ended with a rhetorical flourish: "God has called us to be faithful, not successful!"

"Amen!" responded the assembly. The group then voted to

scrap the evangelistic enterprise.

They had mistakenly concluded that faithfulness and success are diametrically opposed. Unfortunately, that's not an uncommon assumption.

The issues of size and success are inseparable for many pastors. For some bigger is better, with success defined as continued growth in membership, giving, and attendance. The larger the church, they reason, the more people reached with the gospel. These leaders exhibit the creative, pragmatic, and aggressive entrepreneurial spirit that has served American society so well.

Others equate success with "quality" ministry, in particular, effective personal care and nurture. Such leaders worry that increased growth will diminish the close-knit nature of the congregation. Their primary concern is that the sick are visited, the hurting are comforted, and that everyone knows each other's name on Sunday morning.

Which paradigm represents "successful" ministry?

I cannot answer that question concisely. For me success, like a diamond, is multifaceted. The best I can do is show you different facets of the diamond, all of which together make up the luster of pastoral success.

The Difference Church Culture Makes

If we are going to be successful pastors, how our congregations measure success determines to some extent how we must measure it. This varies according to the community we serve.

My older son ministers in a small town of good, solid, reliable people who have been there forever (and will likely remain there forever). One measure of success there is the ability to conduct meaningful funerals. Love and personal nurture top their list of expectations for a pastor. So they measure a pastor by his willingness to visit the elderly, care for the sick and grieving, and continue the programs they've grown to love.

The town faces difficult economic conditions, so the leadership is naturally wary of taking risks. If a pastor can simply maintain the status quo in the face of declining populations, he will be considered a success.

My son is sensitive to that, yet he has managed over a five-year period to help them develop a more dynamic vision for the future. I categorize that as great success.

My youngest son serves in a major metropolitan area. His ministry is primarily to young professionals, and the leaders in his church are movers and shakers, successful businessmen with national and international positions. They tend to have vision, drive, and creativity. Their basic approach to ministry is, "Let's go for it!"

They appreciate my son's drive and initiative, and though he's a young man, they offer him strong support. Given their expectations of a pastor, he too is experiencing success.

My situation differs from both my sons. I minister in what some term a megachurch setting. Most of my elders have joined the church since I became pastor over twenty years ago. As a result, they look to me for leadership initiative. While they function as a strong board, they tend to take their cues from my feelings on a matter. Because we work well together, I consider our relationship a success.

Faithful Despite Fears

One way I measure success is by asking myself three or four times a year, *What did I do, even if I didn't particularly want to, that I knew I should?* Fulfilling one's responsibilities is a major part of success, especially when we overcome apprehensions to do so.

Shortly after I arrived at Elmbrook Church, one of the men largely responsible for bringing me to the church was killed in an accident. Because I had already grown to love him dearly, the idea of performing his funeral was enormously intimidating. What made the situation even more difficult was that all his relatives spoke only German.

But in the providence of God, I had previously ministered in Germany and had gained some comprehension of the language. I was able to conduct some of the service in German. His family seemed deeply touched.

At the end of the day I felt incredible exhilaration. I had faced my fears and fulfilled my biblical responsibility. To me one measure of success is to do what I think is right and good for my people, regardless of my feelings.

Fulfilling Your Primary Roles

Another measure for me has to do with fulfilling my pastoral roles. Sorting through the various roles that we are expected to fulfill successfully is daunting: prophet, counselor, administrator, preacher, teacher, and on and on.

I've found it helpful, though, to keep my job simple. For me, Scripture describes two essential roles, which are valid regardless of the size or location of the church.

● *Pastor/Teacher.* Occasionally I meet pastors who face gridlock with their board. They complain that they can't agree on anything.

I'll often reply by asking, "Well, who is their pastor/teacher?"

"I am," the discouraged minister will reply.

"What are you teaching them?"

They begin to see the point. God has afforded them a weekly platform to shape the thinking of their board and the church in a biblical fashion. Over a long period, sound biblical instruction, taught in a gracious spirit, should diminish disagreements and acrimony.

When I came to Elmbrook, I had neither pastoral training nor previous experience. The board members and I were starting from scratch in our ministry relationship.

"The only thing I know at the moment is a great book on the church called the Bible," I admitted. "I will try to teach it faithfully and accurately. Let's study it together and try to figure out what the church is supposed to be."

I told them I would undoubtedly make mistakes and challenged them to tell me when I was in error. "All I ask," I said, "is that you not criticize me behind my back. Come to me with your

Bible in hand, and we'll discuss the matter." A pastor and congregation can only achieve community to the extent they are prepared to put aside preconceptions and submit every idea to this common point of appeal.

One time, a woman who was upset with me said, "Pastor, I want you to hear me out. But please, don't drag the Bible into this thing!"

I heard her out, but eventually I had to bring the Bible into the conversation. We had no other point of reference.

● *Shepherd.* I measure my success by how well I am tending the flock, and especially in a larger church, by how well I am caring for the leaders who themselves are caring for others. I want to be a patient, caring pastor to my people.

One failure I most regret at Elmbrook had nothing to do with a building project or a doctrinal issue but when I failed in my role as shepherd.

One couple in the church was utterly convinced the church needed a library — immediately. While I did nothing to encourage or discourage their enthusiasm, I doubted whether that was the right time for such an undertaking. We were a new church. A library simply wasn't at the top of my priorities.

But their passion for the project knew no bounds. Time and again the man pressed me to join his card-catalogue crusade. Each time I gently declined. "No, I can't get involved in this."

The man would not be dissuaded. He insisted that I take a public stand in favor of the project. The more I asked him not to push, the more pressure he exerted. My frustration rose.

One day he cornered me and would no longer take no for an answer. He demanded that I throw my support behind the idea and quit rebuffing him. I exploded: "I'm getting angry, very angry with you," I seethed. "This has gone on for weeks. I'm worn out and fed up with your behavior." With that, I turned and walked away in a huff.

As far as I can remember, this is the only time in my two decades at Elmbrook that I have ever spoken so harshly with a parishioner. I still ache when I recall the incident. I hardly displayed the heart of a shepherd. Yet, even as I walked away I thought, *This should not be. Two brothers in Christ should never get in such an adversarial position that they completely lose their tempers.*

That night I went home and began work on a sermon. Sitting with my Bible open and pen ready, I waited, but the words wouldn't come. The spiritual wells within me were pumping only sand. I knew instinctively what was causing the blockage.

So I took out a fresh piece of paper and wrote a letter, apologizing to this man. I took pains to admit how I had acted wrongly and to specify how I felt he had acted improperly. I suggested we meet with a third deacon to iron out the matter, which we eventually did.

Looking back on the incident, it was a failure. My actions were inexcusable, and a fracture in the body of Christ had occurred. Fortunately, it was mended, the couple remained in our church, and today we enjoy superb library facilities, with individuals working on graduate degrees using our resources.

Maintaining Realism, Sustaining Hope

Two dangers exist for pastors when it comes to setting standards for success. One is to shoot for the moon. The other is to throw in the towel.

If I suffer chronic disappointment or disillusionment over my ministry, it might indicate I've been expecting too much, too soon. I need to ask myself the question, *What's disappointing me? Is it the failings of people in the congregation? Or is it my unrealistic expectations?*

For years running, during our annual missions conference, I would go through emotional contortions because so few people seemed interested in world missions. We'd offer splendid speakers and activities all week, but relatively few people would attend, at least compared with Sunday morning attendance.

I just couldn't understand the lack of enthusiasm. After visiting a foreign country, when I boarded a plane for the States I would inevitably turn and say to the missionaries, "Boy, I wish I could stay and help you. There's so much to be done." Then, when I returned home and planned a missions conference, people would stay home and watch a sitcom.

I would get so discouraged about this, my wife, Jill, would dread being around me during missions week. I would make matters worse by scolding the people who did turn out for the conference: "We've got to be more committed to missions!" Fortunately Jill took me aside once and said, "Stuart, don't shout at *them*. They are the ones who showed up."

Gradually, as I gained a bit more sense, I realized that some people will never seek more out of their faith than what's in it for them. The church is comprised exclusively of sinners; unfortunately that includes me. In that sense, it's unwise to expect too much of others or myself. I've resolved not to abandon such people, just as a father doesn't abandon children who are disappointingly slow in development. Neither will I seek to make them perfect according to my time table.

On the other hand, there's a danger of lowering our expectations too far, and thus losing hope. When I meet a stunning setback, it's always a temptation to abandon the project.

As Elmbrook grew, our system of church government, which had worked well when we were a smaller church, became cumbersome and inefficient. So after much thought, I sat down at a typewriter and drafted a proposal to restructure our governing system. The plan flowed effortlessly onto paper, and I couldn't wait to share it with others.

First I presented it to the staff, who wholeheartedly endorsed it. *Wonderful*, I thought. *This is going to sail through the church.*

Next step was the deacons. While the proposal did have its controversial aspects for them (the deacons would be asked to vote themselves into extinction), it seemed like an eminently rational plan they could support.

The deacons responded with passion but not the sort I had hoped for. The discussion degenerated into one of the most difficult board meetings of my entire career.

The chairman of the board, a calm and thoughtful man, said, "I have read your plan, Stuart, and it's positively un-American. Only a Britisher could have written such a document." And that was one of the more charitable statements made that evening! The deacons ripped the document to shreds.

But then one of the board members said, "Any jackass can kick down a barn, but it takes a craftsman to build one. Do we have any craftsmen here tonight?"

The room grew quiet. He went on: "It appears our pastor has made a genuine attempt to deal with a serious problem. Maybe some of us should do the same."

After further discussion, the men responded as any good board would — they created a subcommittee to study the problem. But as a sign of their displeasure, they stacked the committee with those most vehemently opposed to my proposal. The smell of embalming fluid filled the room. I concluded the plan was dead.

I was leaving the next morning for seven weeks of ministry in India, so I asked the board to put one of my associates on the task force. While I was away, the only news I received on the committee's work was a humorous note from my associate added to a letter from Jill: "P.S. We've decided to go with an episcopal form of church government, and you've been unanimously elected archbishop!"

When I returned, I learned to my amazement that the entire subcommittee, having had time to examine the alternatives, now supported the plan 100 percent. We took it to the board, and they passed it unanimously.

Intending to move slowly and involve a large number of people in the discussion, the board mapped out a twelve-month plan to present the new system to the congregation. We scheduled numerous question-and-answer sessions, small group meetings, and educational forums to familiarize the people with the proposal.

Six months into the plan, many said, "Can't we just vote on it right now? Let's do it." In the end only one family voted against the proposal. They left the church but returned six months later.

I had mentally thrown in the towel on this proposal. Fortunately, by God's grace, it rose from the canvas. One facet of success for me, then, is to maintain a realistic but hopeful attitude as I minister.

Looking for Progress

Another facet of success is progress — not perfection but progress.

For instance, success is often measured by a congregation meeting a giving goal. Yet, in most instances, the goals we set are purely arbitrary. Who is to say if a 10 percent or 30 percent increase is too much or too little? The more important question to me is, "Are people progressing in their understanding and expression of biblical stewardship and worship and service?"

The largest Thanksgiving offering we ever received was the result of a presentation by a young woman who had worked on relief trucks in Kenya. She showed her pictures and then brought out a coffee can, filling it with corn to illustrate how little each person had to eat on a daily basis. The people opened their hearts and their wallets that day, and we received a large offering for World Relief, more than we had ever previously given for such a project. It was not the large amount that impressed me but that we had made progress in our ability to give sacrificially.

Take another example: when I finished preaching one series on sexual values, various people came to staff members and said such things as, "We're living together, please help us," or "I've lost my virginity, and I'm feeling desolate." The staff reported a sudden increase in the number of people seeking help in this area. They were responding to the prompting of God's Spirit in their lives, and that kind of progress is a facet of pastoral success.

Diamonds Are Forever

Who is more successful: the pastor who grows a large church or the one who maintains a church in a stagnant area? The pastor who preaches to thousands or the one who lovingly cares for individuals one by one? The pastor who impatiently pushes people to deeper discipleship or the pastor who patiently accepts the shortcomings of his people?

Yes.

Faithfulness, shepherding, teaching, patience, perseverance, growth, progress — these are some of the facets of the diamond of success. Each alone won't bring glory to God, but together they make a lustrous offering to him.

Success is a tapestry of many threads all tightly woven
together by the mysterious working of the Holy Spirit.
— *David Goetz*

Epilogue

Shortly after Robert Stempel resigned as CEO of General Motors in 1992, the *Chicago Tribune* ran an interview with two Ford Motor Company executives.

The interview focused on the troubles at Ford and the search for a new CEO. When asked about the type of person who might successfully lead an organization as complex as Ford Motors, one of the executives replied, "When you look at the whole array of things that have got to be done in a big company these days, it's beyond a product man, it's beyond a financial man. Maybe a clergyman could fit. . . . Professional backgrounds go only a short way to explain what's needed."

Likewise, the many bits of sound advice from our authors only go part way in explaining what's needed to lead a church successfully, another one of life's ambiguous and complex tasks.

Knute Larson, Stuart Briscoe, and Larry Osborne have each brought their distinct personalities, leadership styles, backgrounds, and gifts to their ministries. Each has pastored in unique settings with unique challenges. As each of them admits, their successes are a tapestry of many threads, all tightly woven together by the mysterious working of the Holy Spirit.

"The wind blows wherever it pleases," said Jesus. "You hear its sound, but you cannot tell where it comes from or where it is going. So it is with everyone born of the Spirit."

So it is with every *work* of the Spirit.

We faithfully plant the seed and water it; God blows upon our efforts to give the increase, the success. We risk, fail, persevere, work hard, and apply the principles of effective leadership. And in some magnificent but mysterious way, God honors our efforts.